TOURISM IN 21ST CENTURY

TOURISM IN 21ST CENTURY

Ravindra Verma

CENTRUM PRESS
NEW DELHI-110002 (INDIA)

CENTRUM PRESS
H.O.: 4360/4, Ansari Road, Daryaganj,
New Delhi-110002 (India)
Tel: 23278000, 23261597, 23255577, 23286875
B.O.: No. 1015, Ist Main Road, BSK IIIrd Stage,
IIIrd Phase, IIIrd Block, Bangalore-560085 (INDIA)
Tel: 080-41723429
Email: centrumpress@gmail.com
Visit us at: www.centrumpress.com

Tourism in 21st Century

First Edition, 2010

ISBN 978-93-80540-72-6

PRINTED IN INDIA

Printed at Balaji Offset, Delhi.

Contents

Contents

Preface

The Renaissance or rebirth was a period of divergent thinking that also marked an important stage in the history of travel. New ideas, independent of Christian doctrine spread via books, a product of the printing press and ushered in a period of philosophical change. During the Middle Ages, the church in Europe was a patron of the arts and centre of scholarly activity. The church, even though losing substantial power as a result of the Reformation movement, continued to be a patron of the arts, sponsoring famous Italian artists such as Michelangelo, Leonardo da Vinci and Raphael during the 1500s. Their legacies, represented by their famous works, inspired the Grand Tour, which reached its height of popularity in the 1700s. The artistic accomplishments of this period continue to form part of the European travel experience today.

The Grand Tour is English in origin, and it was primarily a 'finishing school' for the sons of the British elite. The purpose of the Grand Tour which for some lasted over three years, was exposure to the cultural attractions of the European mainland. While the primary reason for travel during the Middle Ages were trade and religious pilgrimages, the focus now shifted to attaining cultural enrichment. Tour participants were accompanied by a mentor and guardian. They were expected not only to observe the arts, literature, music, science and other cultural refinements of Europe, but were expected to return home with an increased ability to utilize the knowledge gained in their travels. The purpose of the Grand Tour eventually evolved from one of learning for the young to one of sensual pleasure for all ages. Some maintain that the Grand Tour continues to exist today as evidenced by the pilgrimage of North American travellers to the cultural centre of Europe.

The origins of a modern tourism industry – cultural tourism in particular – are believed to have begun with the Grand Tour. Many of the major cities of Europe (e.g. Paris, Milan and Rome) developed superior hotels and service for their guests. Stays in each capital were long by today's standard, as travel was still relatively risky and laborious.

The book examines the current trends in international tourism along with emerging opportunities and challenges in the field.

—Ravindra Verma

1

Tourism Marketing Strategies

The tourism consumer is the critical judge of successful marketing and public relations activities. In today's increasingly competitive marketing environment there has been a shift from traditional marketing techniques towards more aggressive and varied approaches to marketing and communication.

The change from transactional to relationship management in marketing over the past fifty years has been marked by improvements in consumer satisfaction and client recommendation of repeat purchase of products and services.

In the twenty first century informed and discerning clients dictate whether the brand and image are coherent and the recognition by organisations of the power of their brand and its image is a central theme to contextualise the marketing activity.

Today's brands are often built with effective PR campaigns and then maintained through a blend of marketing and PR tactics.

The impact of the Internet is having profound impact upon PR and Marketing practices enabling PR practitioners to conduct two way communications in order to maintain and enhance customer relationships.

Indicative Content

- Marketing strategies in the hospitality and tourism sector
- Creating and developing customer loyalty
- Network and relationship marketing

- Brand identity and strategy
- Strategic customer relations
- Viral and guerilla marketing
- Effectiveness of e-marketing.

Innovation Management – An Indian Experience

Innovation has been instrumental for technology upgradation leading to productivity, growth and international competitiveness of the industry. The technology development, its further adaptation and application have never been the straightforward process.

A successful technology innovation requires a strong interactive mechanism complete with the feedback loop for various stakeholders viz. industry, extraneous knowledge sources, inspection & certification agencies and most importantly, the users or the market. However, the problems become acute in rapidly changing technological and economic environment.

Technology innovation is key to the survival of small & medium enterprises (SMEs) in India. The SMEs play a crucial role in Indian industry. They constitute 15 million units, contribute 6-7% of total GDP and employ 30 million people. More importantly, 40% of the industrial production in India comes from the SMEs. Finance is the key driver for innovation process for the SMEs and the cost of funds should be attractive enough for them for investing in projects involving technological risks. They are often beset by multi-faceted problems, which include the following :

- Availability of quality raw materials
- Inadequate infrastructure facilities
- Availability of skilled labour
- Access to market
- Development of in-house technical & managerial capabilities
- Long product development cycle
- Extraneous knowledge support
- Lack of standards & certification process in some cases their internal resistance to change....

In order to mitigate such problems and to effect a seamless technology development process for subsequent commercialization, the requirement of a well-defined strategy had strongly been felt by the Government. Four decades of planned development have elevated India to a stage, where the country can show some remarkable strength in modern technologies for achieving development goals.

There exists a chain of national laboratories, specialized R&D agencies in defence, atomic energy & space, Indian Institutes of Technology (IITs), universities & other academic institutions of higher learning, which are capable of providing world-class expertise, technically trained manpower and technology support to the industry.

The institutes have been pursuing application-oriented research, which led to amassing an excellent knowledge pool. However, the extent of knowledge flow from such centres of excellence to the industry for its actual exploitation for the prototype development and reaching out to market has been limited. Various policy interventions were directed and organizational structures along with the fiscal incentives were designed by the Government from time to time to bridge the gap.

Innovation Management Approaches

Keeping in view of the critical need for technology innovation, *Technology Information, Forecasting and Assessment Council (TIFAC)* was conceptualized as a unique knowledge networking institution in India for facilitating novel technology developments for the key sectors of economy. TIFAC was established as an autonomous organization under the aegis of Department of Science & Technology, Government of India.

As a follow-up of a detailed sectoral analysis coupled with the technology assessment exercise, composites were identified as an important performing material with a wide array of applications touching a large number of people from different walks of life.

The increasing demand for materials with higher strength-to-weight ratio has led to the cognizance of composites. The composite technology of a matrix reinforced with man-made fibres such as glass, Kevlar, carbon etc. after meeting the challenges of aerospace sector has cascaded down for catering to the industrial and domestic applications.

Composite structures are becoming increasingly significant in a number of novel applications in engineering fields. They meet stringent requirement such as performance at high temperature, pressure, corrosive environment or high stress.

Due to their lightweight coupled with high strength, composites can replace wooden & heavy metallic parts in transportation (automobiles & railways) thus directly contributing to energy savings. The usage of composites for bio-medical applications can be a boon to the patients for reducing the drudgery of carrying heavy weight.

Assessing the status of composite industry in India, it was felt that there was an ardent need to boost the usage of composites through indigenous design capability, incorporation of advanced fabrication technologies, product development & testing.

Any major impact in the sector seemed unlikely unless it was taken up as a mission mode programme with commitment from the Government. The *Advanced Composites Mission,* initiated by TIFAC, aimed to promote various composite applications in components for railways & automobiles, construction materials, medical appliances, chemical & marine applications and others. Important strategic inputs and specific products were developed for commercialization under the mission mode programme.

In line with the above, setting up centres of excellence for assistance in design, prototype development, product evaluation and also for technology transfer & absorption by the Indian composite industry were identified as a priority areas. The Mission had set up two composite design & development centres viz. RV-TIFAC Composite Design Centre (CDC), Bangalore and Composite Technology Centre at IIT-Madras, Chennai. Manpower was recognized as another key factor for development of composite technology.

The Mission had launched a major project in partnership with the Central Institute of Plastics Engineering & Technology (CIPET),

Chennai for developing courses & curricula for training persons in composite technology.

In view of the application potential of composites, a fast paced indigenous product development & its induction was felt necessary for important sectors. Other aspects such as usage of natural fibre (jute, sisal, pineapple, banana, coir...) in composites, development of new fibre & resin system, recyclability/reusability of composites and their effective disposal were also considered important thrust areas.

The Advanced Composites Mission had experimented with varied innovation management models for the aforesaid development of composite applications. They are explained hereunder:

Model - I : Laboratory Based Technology Development

Initially the projects were conceived by the Mission wherein the technology development activities would be undertaken by a national R&D lab. The projects would be financially supported by TIFAC and the participating industry; the funds were required to be released to the R&D lab working on the project. The industry partner was required to upscale the technology for commercialization once the product gets developed successfully.

Two projects were conceptualized in this mode in partnership with a defence research laboratory. The products targeted for development were high-technology applications warranting extremely critical testing & certification regime. In fact, the criticality of testing requirement was not assessed properly prior to project conceptualization.

The project evaluation & monitoring mechanism did not foresee any involvement of users or certification agencies. Thus the product development process distanced itself from the market and when the prototypes were developed successfully, their induction by the users was difficult.

The participating industry was not much inclined to the aforesaid mechanism, especially for providing funding support to the R&D lab. As the lab was the centre of all actions, the industry had perceived that they were extraneous to the entire development process. Moreover, all the assets were being created within the lab premises with the financial support from TIFAC and the industry– this was not an attractive proposition for the industry.

As the project involved very sophisticated level of technology development followed by critical testing procedures, the development cycle experienced many bottlenecks and delays. The industry partner lost interest in the project in due course as the project showed no promise for possibility of early commercialization.

Model – II : Lab Oriented Technology Development with Extraneous Industry Involvement

The experience of taking up the technology development activities at the R&D lab did not meet with much success as explained above. This prompted the Mission to involve the user agencies more proactively in the project to the extent of sharing the financial assistance along with TIFAC. In this new approach, the financial support was still extended to the national R&D labs and the industry partners were not directly involved in the project.

The knowledge partner (R&D lab), identified for the project, had sufficient expertise in product design & development, selection of raw materials and necessary product testing. The user agency had identified the product to be developed under the project and shown keen interest in participating in TIFAC mode of project implementation.

They took a very active part in the project by extending financial assistance to the R&D lab to the tune of 50% of the total project cost.

The user agency helped in finalizing the design approach, carrying out necessary in-house testing & field trials for prototype approval. Such an involvement by the user agency was expected to play a catalytic role for early induction of the product. On successful technology development and transfer of technology licensing rights to the user agency, they also ensured repayment of funds to facilitating agency, TIFAC.

As technology facilitator, TIFAC had extended financial support to the tune of 50% of the total project cost to the R&D lab for undertaking developmental project.

This technology innovation approach was followed in *development of FRP sleepers* for railway girder bridges. The Research & Development Establishment (Engineers), Pune was identified as the R&D lab and Research, Design & Standards Organization (RDSO), Lucknow acted on behalf of the user agency (Indian Railways) for the project.

Composite sleepers were designed to replace the existing wooden and steel channel sleepers on girder bridges. The sleepers were successfully tested at RDSO & Structural Engineering Research Centre (SERC), Chennai and finally accepted by the Indian Railways due to excellent vibration absorption, extended life cycle, considerable weight saving and improved maintainability.

However, there was no direct involvement of the industry in the entire development process. While the R&D lab designed the product and finalized its fabrication process, they could not develop the prototype for lack of advanced fabrication equipment. Hence, the technology was required to be transferred to competent composite fabricators with good technical capabilities for prototype development and its large-scale replication in case of commercial induction.

Though industries were identified at later stage for the prototype development, they were not fully geared to adopt and absorb the technology from the R&D lab. This led to delay in entire product development cycle.

Model – III : Industry Centric Innovation

Based on earlier experiences of mixed successes, a new strategy was adopted and the Mission policies were reoriented considerably for ensuring an active involvement of the industry in the entire process of technology development. It was realized that successful technology development model should be industry centric, keeping the industry as the centre of all the actions namely, product conceptualization & design, assets creation for prototype development, testing and finally large-scale replication for wider induction. This called for extraneous knowledge support from the leading centres of excellence across the country and brought the industries closer for technology absorption, development & dissemination. The knowledge partner provided design support to the industry in terms of engineering drawings, preparation of data sheets, reports and advice on raw material selection, fabrication process, testing etc. for successful development of the prototype composite product. The programme involved faculty members from the renowned institutes such as IITs.

In order to reduce technology development cycle, the Mission started involving key persons from the user groups, certifying agencies etc. in the project monitoring committees for effective project management, technology support, product evaluation etc.

The Committee provided a right mix of expertise on design, process, machine/equipment, testing & quality assurance. Such user oriented project monitoring has been the cornerstone of project management and it has greatly helped in improving the market reach of composite products and their acceptance in the shortest possible time. Thus, the projects were more focused with clear time bound objectives and most of them were completed with successful product development and user acceptance.

With the modified Mission priorities, the Technology Development Assistance was extended directly by TIFAC to the industries on repayable basis. The major thrust was on generating market-driven projects with potential applications in sectors such as railways, telecom, building & construction, biomedical etc. With this change in focus, industry's participation was intensified & many new projects with novel composite applications were initiated.

Supported by the Technology Development Assistance from TIFAC, the industries had set up advanced fabrication system in-house and testing & quality control facilities for manufacturing composite products meeting the international standards & quality norms. This has contributed significantly to the up gradation of composite technology for a wide array of applications. This greatly contributed to the capability improvement for the industry and generated confidence among the users in product acceptance.

Achievement Highlights

The Advanced Composites Mission made substantial contribution towards development and growth of indigenous composite products. With the evolution of optimally workable technology innovation mechanism, a large number of projects was initiated in partnership with the Indian composite industry and academia.

The composite technology originally developed for the aviation and space sectors has started reaching common market in a cost-effective manner.

The Mission was successful in bringing a culture of technology development towards commercialization especially for the technology starved SMEs. In view of the achievements and successes of the Advanced Composites Mission, the Advanced Composites Programme was taken up by TIFAC as a regular activity. Some of the products developed under the programme for different sectors are highlighted as follows:

- Composites in transportation – gear-case for diesel locomotives, energy efficient axial flow radiator cooling fans for diesel locomotive,
- modular toilets for railway coaches, main & sliding doors for railway passenger coaches,
- interiors for drivers' cabin in diesel locomotive for railways, interiors for railway passenger coaches,
- Sky bus coach for Konkan Railway,
- bracket assembly for overhead railway electric traction,
- houseboat, components for high-end passenger buses, filament wound road tankers,
- high speed boats Industrial composite products – double-wall vessels for chemical storage, axial flow fans (for cooling towers, textile mill dehumidifiers, air heat exchangers, mine ventilation), pressure vessels, filament wound pipes & pipe-fittings, filament wound venturi scrubber, CNG cylinders for automobiles, grids/gratings for chemical industry,

- modular acoustic enclosures for DG sets o Building & infrastructure
- multi-purpose modular housing system o Biomedical application
- below knew artificial limbs for physically handicapped, carbon fibre external ring fixator as an orthopaedic appliance o Natural fibre composites
- jute-coir boards as wood substitutes, bamboo laminates for flooring tiles and shutters, jute composite components for footwear.

Select Case Studies

The Advanced Composites programme has proven itself as an efficient delivery mechanism imparting excellent economic advantage in terms of creating material with superior properties, substituting scarce materials, developing value-added applications and most importantly business volume generation.

The industry partners for the programme have achieved strong and profitable growth (+10% to 30% of sales increase per year generating 10% to 40% of return on capital employed). The following section discusses select case studies concerning technology development projects with the details on the need for developing such products, process of development and the outcomes.

Composite Modular Toilets for Railway Passenger Coaches

Indian Railways have been striving to improve passenger comfort and amenities with better reliability. It was felt that the toilets at the passenger coaches needed gross improvement in aesthetics and functionality.

The toilets, presently built integral with the coaches, are not at all aesthetically appealing. The toilet floors are provided with faulty gradient and thus they are prone to water accumulation and heavy leakages.

The leakage from the toilet floors corrodes the undercarriage structural elements. All these called for frequent maintenance and expensive repairs especially for the undercarriage. In such a scenario, the toilets made of composites with a moulded floor could be the right step for preventing the leakage and corrosion. This has been the collective view of the Carriage Directorate of RDSO-Lucknow and ICF-Chennai of Indian Railways.

In view of the above, the development of composite modular toilet units of improved aesthetics and maintainability was identified as one of the priority projects for Indian Railways. In line with the identified requirement, the project was launched by TIFAC in partnership with *Hindustan Fibre Glass Works, Vadodara* with technology support from *IIT-Bombay.*

Apart from the involvement of Industrial Design Centre (IDC) of IIT-Bombay for improved aesthetics, ergonomics and usability, support from Department of Aerospace Engineering was also sought in terms of structural design of composite toilets, reinforcement lay-up, mould design & fabrication, selection of suitable raw materials, testing & mechanical characterization and quality assurance norms for fabrication.

In order to bring in the right expertise and assistance for performance evaluation & guidance, the Advanced Composites Programme involved experts from various units of railways such as Railway Board, RDSO, RCF, ICF etc in the project evaluation committee.

The composite modular toilet unit was developed with four parts: the flooring trough, one L-shaped sidewall, one C-shaped sidewall & roof. All these composite components were fabricated by resin transfer moulding (RTM) process; such large components were fabricated by RTM for the first time in India.

The modularity in construction for the toilet helped in taking its each part inside the compartment through the main door and they could be assembled in situ within a short time. The composite toilet unit has been light in weight, corrosion resistant, fire retardant; it has longer life with easy maintainability. Salient features of the toilets are as follows:

- Composite sandwich door, lipped with pultruded composite frame on all four sides of the door

- Ventilation provided in the toilet on the side-wall and at the lower part of the door
- Sacrificial PVC flooring with improved anti-skid and anti-abrasion properties used above the composite trough
- Concealed type Ki-tech flexible conduits with aluminium core encased within two HDPE layers for longer life with virtually no maintenance and required contours during fixing
- Light-weight 110 V DC fan, one CFL light (110 V), push type flush valve, longer vertical handle for support on right side of the pan etc. incorporated in the Indian style toilet unit.

Various other features such as space for toiletries, mug space & its mounting arrangement, taps for washbasin & near pan, wall protector, mirror positions etc. were finalized for the composite toilet unit.

Four toilet units were fitted into an AC-II tier coach of Mumbai-Delhi Rajdhani Express. The coach with composite toilets was inaugurated by Dr. R Chidambaram, Chairman-TIFAC, on October 20, 2001, at Carriage Repair Workshop of Western Railway, Mumbai, in the presence of a galaxy of senior officials from Indian Railways.

Based on the initial field trials, composite toilets were inducted by the Indian Railways for many important trains. The project bagged the Certificate of Merit under the National Award for Excellence in Consultancy Services–2001 awarded to IDC/IIT-Bombay by the Consultancy Development Centre of DSIR, Govt. of India. The technology for composite toilet units was licensed to nine composite fabricators due to its large demand by the Indian Railways.

Composite Interiors for Driver's Cabin in Diesel Locomotive

There are two driver seats along with the consoles as mirror images at two ends of the driver's cabin for diesel locomotives. The driver's cabin accommodates the tool kit, almirah, panels for various instruments & control etc. The cabin in its present design is too cramped for free movement & comfort for the operators.

The consoles appear cluttered with not so well designed placement of several dials & gauges. The Indian Railways have been seriously contemplating ways and means for an ergonomic improvement of driver's cabin interiors for diesel locomotives along with an improved aesthetic appeal.

In view of the long felt needs by the Indian Railways for modernizing the driver's cabin interiors, the project was launched with *M/s. Black Burn Co. Pvt. Ltd., Kolkata* with technology support from *IIT-Bombay*. The project aimed at developing the driver's cabin interiors for diesel locomotives using composite components thereby improving the aesthetics and ergonomics for improved user comfort.

The Industrial Design Centre (IDC) of IIT-Bombay helped in prototype design & development, preparation of various design drawings, fabrication of full-scale prototype etc. For a user oriented development approach, the experts from Railway Board, RDSO, DLW, DLMW and Western Railway were inducted in the project review & monitoring activities.

The new design of the cabin as evolved has addressed appropriate paneling, comfortable seats, clear visibility while operating the locomotive, proper arrangement of gauges, provision of space for tools & kits etc. The problems of heat & sound insulation were also addressed while developing the cabin interiors.

In addition, the safety features such as increase in roof height inside the cabin, scientific illumination of the cabin, ergonomically correct placement of various instruments, indication regarding driver's attentiveness were all addressed in the driver's cabin. The modifications as suggested by the users were incorporated at various stages.

The design of interiors comprising wall & roof panels, flooring, console panel etc. was carried out based on human body clearances, space requirement for ingress & outgress, tool box dimensions, minimum space for drivers' belongings etc. The side panels & console panels were given an off-white granular granite finish. The roof panels were painted white to improve the interior light condition.

A cupboard was provided at the short-hood side to accommodate tools and other accessories. The space between the consoles was increased considerably to faciiitate free movement of personnel and height adjusted to ensure eyeball contact between driver & assistant.

Openable hatches were provided below the console desk for access to the cables, gauges & other mountings. The roof comprised of two arched panels on either side and a central panel to accommodate lighting fixtures with shadow light. The set of wires/ cables feeding the two console panels were laid below the floor.

The floor of the cabin was made in three-piece modular composite panels for accessing underneath. Wide openable hatches were provided at the long-hood side for access to various MCBs/ switches/knobs, gauges and other accessories. The existing metal door was cladded with composite panels inside and a standard lock was provided.

On approval of the full-scale mock-up of driver's cabin, the drivers' cabins of two diesel locomotives (WDM-2A) were furnished with composite interiors at Ratlam loco-shed of Western Railway by Black Burn & Co. The users' feedback from the field trials of the diesel locomotives furnished with composite interiors has been quite encouraging.

The diesel loco maintenance unit from Ratlam loco-shed had inferred that the newly furnished diesel loco driver's cabin has created quite a conducive workspace. STR covering the technical specifications, design drawings, fabrication process and testing requirements for the newly developed composite interiors has been finalized by RDSO and efforts are underway in inducting them on large-scale by Indian Railways.

Composite Houseboat for Tourism

Originally known as 'kettuvallom' and used for carrying rice & other grains in the villages dotting along the backwaters of Kerala, houseboat is a rather recent innovation positioned as the unique attraction for an already thriving tourism industry in the state. A houseboat can be the ultimate statement in luxury.

The tour operators in Kerala have experimented with many variants of the houseboat. While the standard houseboat is equipped with two or three bedrooms, some have been made into a honeymooner's haven with one large bedroom.

Some have also been designed with a double-deck configuration with top deck being used for conference and the lower one serving as the dining hall.

Conceptualized around 10 years ago, houseboat in the backwaters of Kerala has become quiet a rage with a current population of around 250 and about 15-20 boats being built every year for catering to an ever rising demand, houseboat is traditionally made of resinous wood and it takes 8-10 trees (70-80 years old) to build one.

Apart from denuding the forest cover, building a traditional houseboat is extremely manpower intensive and nearly 40 man months of skilled labour are required to shape it up.

The wooden hull is highly prone to decay due to its continuous contact with water calling for regular tarring of the hull and frequent outages of the houseboat. The superstructure outer surface thatched with woven bamboo mat requires replacement every year due to an excessive fungal attack in a moist environment.

Thus the cost of maintenance becomes quite prohibitive for the houseboat and for the tourists to enjoy that 'ultimate in luxury' the cost of occupancy rises!

The introduction of diesel engines into houseboats has made them economical to operate, but it has become uncomfortable due to noise and vibrations. All these made houseboat a good candidate to be developed in composite for corrosion resistance, ease in fabrication and maintenance free service.

The development of *composite houseboat* for tourism was taken up as a project under the Advanced Composites Programme of TIFAC for improved aesthetics, boat stability, comfort level and maintainability.

The project was launched in partnership with *M/s. Samudra Shipyard Pvt. Ltd., Aroor near Cochin*. A multi-agency approach was adopted for seeking expertise in hull design, testing, fabrication assistance, design of superstructure, interiors, amenities etc. *NGN Composites-Chennai,* a consulting agency working in composites technology development, had assisted in mechanical design & fabrication of hull, deck & superstructure.

The technology support from NGN Composites included design and development of patterns and moulds for boat hull & superstructure and quality control during fabrication process. The Dept. of Ocean Engineering of IIT-Madras had provided hydrodynamic design of boat hull, bulkheads, ballasts and conducted the necessary tests for boat stability.

The *Industrial Design Centre (IDC) of IIT-Bombay* had extended design support for developing a superstructure with improved space utilization of the available envelop, aesthetics and ergonomics of the living area with the detailed design of bedrooms, toilets, dining area, lounge, kitchen etc. including design of panels, partitions & other interiors. The important milestone of IDC's contribution has been modular design approach of the entire superstructure.

The scaled down (1:17) version of composite hull was designed & fabricated by IIT-Madras and tested for its hydrodynamic stability in their towing tank. The model hull behaviour was studied at various speeds and the hull profile was determined for scaling up.

Finally the full-scale hull size measuring 26 m long x 4.50 m wide x 1.50 m deep was firmed up. IIT-Madras has also designed the propeller profile, shaft & the drive mechanism for the propulsion system.

The sandwich hull with polyurethane foam core was fabricated in composite. The decking for the houseboat has always been a problem area with a whole lot of wooden planks being used in the conventional ones. This problem was addressed by using moulded resin infused composite gratings, developed under another TIFAC project. The gratings were vertically supported along the centre line of the hull.

For superstructure, efforts were made to retain the traditional look with curved wall profiles and pagoda type roofing. The entire superstructure was made into five modular parts requiring only three moulds for fabricating the half modules.

The pagoda style roofing with flat false ceiling inside the bedrooms provides good thermal insulation due to the available air gap. The superstructure was configured to accommodate two bedrooms each measuring 4.00 m x 3.50 m with large windows, attached toilets, a 1.0-m wide passage, living room with open deck, kitchen, crew toilet etc.

Hard wood like bamboo composite flooring tiles, developed under a TIFAC project, were used in the bedrooms. The houseboat components such as the hull, deck and the superstructure consumed about 19.20 tons of composites, thus making the houseboat one of the largest composite products in the country.

A 104 HP Cummins diesel engine, used for the propulsion system, was housed inside the hull with anti-vibration mountings. An acoustic barrier in the form of high resilience foam was used in the engine enclosure for a noise free operation.

A 10-KVA DG set was installed inside the hull for the power back-up when the engine is not in operation as the boat is anchored during the night. Polymer concrete ballasts weighing 1.50 tons were added inside the hull to improve boat stability.

Three bulkheads were provided in the hull to isolate the hull puncture and water leakage. The composite houseboat has been operational in the backwaters of Kerala and its services are being enjoyed by the tourists on regular basis.

The composite houseboat has been a small step in technology development but this would go a long way in saving the environment. Involvement of the multi-agency expertise and a user-oriented approach have been instrumental in reducing the product development cycle limiting the entire exercise to under one year.

While boat building in India has been a traditional activity, it is now important to introduce new materials such as composites and processes such as vacuum infusion technique. With very long coast lines along the peninsula, large natural inland water bodies and long rivers, development of composite boats of various forms

& functions in India would certainly assume importance and attract investment in the near future.

Jute-Coir Composites as Wood Substitute

Natural fibre composites have gained interest in the last decade, especially in the housing & construction sector. In view of the indigenous wood supply for plywood industry having been stopped virtually and with increasing landed cost of imported plywood veneers, the natural fibre composite boards were required to be developed without compromising any properties and simultaneously offering good value to the customers. Value-added composites from natural fibre could be excellent revenue generation proposition for the farmers.

Keeping in view the aforesaid objectives, the project was launched in collaboration with *M/s. Natura Fibretech Pvt. Ltd., Bangalore* for the development of jute-coir composite boards with face veneer (oriented jute) and coir/rubber wood veneers inside. A thin layer of jute fibres impregnated with phenolic resin was used as the face veneer for improved aesthetics and to impart a wood like finish.

The orientation & uniformity of jute fibre improved with carding and this also helped in better penetration of resin into the fibre. As colour of face veneer is important for appearance, a mixture of brown & bleached jute would resemble the natural wood. The thin jute face veneer, supported by a craft paper sheet, serves as an impervious layer resulting in reduced consumption of paints while finishing the board.

For inside veneers, needle felted coir mat was impregnated with specially formulated coir compatible phenol-formaldehyde resin with reasonably fast curing properties. The waste rubber wood veneers were also impregnated with phenolic resin.

For the boards containing rubber wood, the resin impregnated wood veneers are arranged as intermediate layers during assembly. The assembling is carried out by placing oriented jute layer at two outer faces with semi-cured coir felt sheets inside.

The number of coir and rubber wood layers to be used as inside veneers depends on desired thickness of the finished board.

The assembly of various layers is compression moulded and cured in multi-plated hydraulic press with continuous monitoring of temperature, pressure & time.

In the project, 80% of the material used in the composite were renewable natural fibres such as jute and coir. The coir fibre contains 46 % lignin as against 39% in teakwood.

Therefore, it has improved resistance against rotting under wet and dry conditions and has better tensile strength. Similarly lower cellulose content in coir (43%) as against 63% in wood makes it more durable than teakwood. Several applications were identified for jute-coir composite boards: building & construction, furniture industry, transportation etc.

The project evaluation committee was constituted considering the product acceptance, usage & induction by involving experts from BMTPC, CPWD, RDSO, IJIRA. The characteristics of natural fibre composite boards are as follows:

- Attractive natural look; it can be painted, polished or laminated at will
- Water proof with minimum surface absorption Economical
- Strong and rigid
- Fire retardant
- Environment-friendly
- Can be nailed, screwed and cut sharply.

The product range developed under the project, comprises coirply (jute+coir+rubber wood waste) boards as plywood substitute and *natural fibre reinforced panel* (jute+coir composites) as MDF substitute. The jute-coir boards as MDF & plywood substitutes was tested satisfactorily at IPIRTI-Bangalore as per relevant IS codes. The performance of jute-coir composite boards has proven superior to plywood & MDF boards.

Typical MDF boards do not prove well on the grounds of moisture absorption & screw holding strength. Detailed evaluation of the jute-coir board samples was also carried out by RDSO & ICF for their applications as berth backings in railway coaches; the results conformed to the railways' requirements.

In fact, with sustained efforts by the Programme Scientists & the industry partner, the Indian Railways had approved the product for coach interiors. Indian Railways inducted the jute-coir boards (8 ft. x 4 ft. x 6 mm thick) on large-scale for berth backing at ICF-Chennai.

The Bureau of Indian Standards (BIS) has brought out the relevant standards (IS 14842 : 2000) for coir veneer boards and the product developed under the project conforms to the codes.

These natural materials have all the properties required for a general purpose board and can be used in place of plywood or MDF boards for partitioning, false ceiling, surface panelling, roofing, furniture, cupboards, wardrobes etc.

With active pursuance of the Advanced Composites Programme, the product made excellent in-roads to railways, CPWD, BSNL, Govt. of Karnataka and others.

Apart from the domestic market, the product also enjoys very good technology transfer possibilities in the international arena especially in the coir producing countries in Africa and South-East Asia. As the product is derived from fast renewable natural resources, the project does serve its basic objective of saving forest.

Development of Artificial Limbs for Physically Handicapped

Artificial limbs can be quite effective in restoring the normal movement for victims of trauma, accidents and other amputees. In addition to replacing lost functions, artificial limbs can result in cosmetic improvements for the patient and help build the self-confidence.

The artificial limb developed initially in the world has been an exoskeleton, which was more of a cosmetic replacement rather than a functional one. Though these appear like natural limbs, they cannot impart normal gait to a person.

The conventional exoskeleton types of artificial limbs are heavy in weight and are not at all comfortable for the patients. Subsequently efforts were directed internationally to develop endoskeleton type of artificial limbs. Modern artificial limbs have come a long way from the old wooden exoskeleton type of artificial leg. The endoskeleton replicates the functionality of bones for load bearing and involves proper mechanical joints for normal gait. Advanced endoskeleton type artificial limbs are now made from modern lightweight materials and often-incorporate electronic & pneumatic mechanisms.

In India, commonly used artificial legs are exoskeleton type made of high-density polyethylene. Though the imported endoskeleton types of limbs are available in India, they are very expensive.

As physical deformities aggravate the economic woes of the victims in our country, it called for an indigenous development to restore the functional normalcy of physically challenged people at an affordable price.

On assessing the present scenario towards improving design, functional needs & aesthetics of the artificial limbs in India to cater to societal needs a project on developing *'composite artificial limbs for physically handicapped'* was launched in collaboration with *Mohana Orthotics & Prosthetic Centre, Chennai* with technology support from *IIT-Madras* and *Madras Institute of Technology, Chennai* in terms of design, prototype development and complete testing of composite limbs.

The below-the-knee endoskeleton artificial limbs developed under the project were lighter in weight and better appearance than ever before with improved gait for the patients.

This below-the-knee endoskeleton limb consists of five parts: a composite tubular structure fabricated by filament winding of glass fibre in epoxy matrix, top & bottom connectors made by injection moulding of glass filled nylon, a polyurethane foot with composite keel embedded in it and a polypropylene socket to accommodate the amputee stump.

The socket is patient specific and does not create any problems like pressure sores even for diabetic patients. All the five parts and the socket are adjustable to meet individual requirements and to take care of static & dynamic alignment patterns.

A very innovative design approach was adopted for designing the composite keel, fabricated by compression moulding, for providing improved strength & flexibility in the foot piece. Provision was made to take care of the alignment when they were fitted to the patient.

The new polyurethane foot allowed a foot to press and spring on the ground very much like a real foot. 3-D modelling of the endoskeleton with all the embedded components considering actual properties of various materials was carried out. A simulated endurance test was conducted for 5-year service life of the artificial limb considering average stance duration of 0.5 seconds for normal gait and three hours walking time per day thus testing the limb for around 40 million cycles.

The indigenously developed artificial limb has high modulus, long-term dimensional stability, high fatigue resistance, long-term bio-stability excellent abrasion resistance and bio-compatibility. They look like a natural foot, it is sturdy, durable, waterproof and made of locally available material.

The unique design of this composite limb permits walking, cycling, climbing and even driving a vehicle by a person physically challenged otherwise. A whole lot of innovative technology inputs from MIT was instrumental in developing a user friendly & world-class artificial limb with excellent market potential in India and abroad.

Such indigenously developed below-knee artificial limb cost maximum Rs.3,500/- only as against Rs.40,000/- for the imported ones. The endoskeleton type below-knee artificial limb developed by Mohana Orthotics was awarded the prestigious *National R&D Award 2001* by the Department of Scientific & Industrial Research (DSIR), Govt. of India.

Conclusion

The Advanced Composites Programme has been a truly successful experiment in innovation management in Indian context. Each of the earlier described innovation management approaches as adopted under the programme had their efficacies in specific cases. The first approach of laboratory based technology development exercise was typically suitable for the composite applications involving cutting edge technologies.

The expertise as well as the facilities for application development were available only at a defence lab and such projects could not be initiated by an industry on its own. In the second approach for the technology development, the prototypes were developed and tested successfully.

This was due to the financial stake of the user agencies and their complete involvement in the project especially for facilitating the testing & product certification. The entire technology development exercise could have been faster if the industry were involved right from the early stages of the project and not only for the prototype development.

Building on the experiences of earlier approaches of innovation management practices, the optimal mechanism of industry centric innovation had emerged with the promise of near-term deliverables. Around 30 projects were conceptualized following this approach and a large majority of them were concluded successfully with the products reaching out to the users.

The attributes such as attractive scheme of financial assistance, technological risk sharing and knowledge-based project monitoring by experts coupled with the market intervention by reaching to the user agencies had all helped the programme to record its achievements in a short span. The programme had roped in a good number of academicians with excellent expertise in product design & fabrication and effectively utilized their knowledge in realizing the applications.

The networking by the programme among the academia/ research institutions, standards & certifying agencies as well as the experts from the actual users has gone a long way in reducing the product development cycles.

Different Dimensions of Indian Tourism Industry

The tourism industry has two major aspects:

1. Tourism
2. Travel.

Tourism includes various types, like medical tourism, health tourism, spiritual tourism and rural tourism. The travel segment includes various tour operators and other travel agencies. There are a number or emerging dimensions of tourism. These include:

1. Medical Tourism: Indian tourism is aiming to promote its allopathic treatment as a tourist attraction. Medical tourism tends to provide world-class treatment at low price and is gaining worldwide acceptance. Doctors and other medical experts are organizing health camps and other general awareness programs. The vast array of health care services includes ayurveda, yoga, naturopathy, meditation, spas and many more.
2. Spiritual Tourism: India has a rich heritage of cultures and religions. Hinduism, Buddhism, Christianity, Islam, Jainism have lived here for centuries. There is so much mental pressure and disturbance all over the world that people are looking forward to find solace. India is being represented as a destination for spiritual tourism. Spiritual tourism includes all the religions, religious places associated with them, and emotional attachment and beliefs attached to these centres. Thus, through religious tourism there is a sincere effort to bring better understanding among various communities, nations and thus foster global unity.
3. Rural Tourism: Real India is rural India. Almost 74% of the population is in rural areas. For the development of rural India, government is promoting rural tourism. Rural tourism showcases the rural life in India, the art, culture and heritage, the nature and wild life and various other aspects of rural India. The rural India has a great potential to attract foreign tourists. The rural tourism helps in improving lives of rural people and maintaining the quality of environment.
4. Adventurous Tourism: India is an incredible destination for adventures. The snow capped Himalayas, erratic streams, safaris, etc all add to its natural glory. Water sports, elephant safari, mountaineering, skiing, gliding, trekking, river rafting, etc are breath-taking opportunities for adventurous people. Ladakh, the Garwal hills, the

Himachal hills, Darjeeling, Goa, Lakshadweep, Andaman and Nicobar Islands, are some of the places that offer adventure tourism.

5. MICE Tourism: MICE (meetings, incentives, conferences and exhibitions) is associated with business travelers. It caters to various forms of business meetings, international conferences and conventions, events and exhibitions. India is gaining pace to become an ideal MICE destination due to the flourishing business here. The MICE industry converts the annual business meetings and conferences into a glamorous and enjoyable event for the delegates and attendants. To develop business tourism in India, some renowned MICE centres are already established. The Ashok (New Delhi), Hyderabad International Convention Centre (Hyderabad), Le Meridien (Cochin), Delhi International Expo Centre (Noida) are some of them.
6. Eco Tourism: People are visiting India to unravel the secrets of nature. Eco tourism (also known as nature tourism) relates to nature and its attractiveness so that the visitors experience it in its pristine settings. Eco tourism attracts domestic as well as international tourists towards the magnificent ancient cities, hill stations, remote villages, desert areas and wildlife centuries and parks in India. It is the fastest growing sector of Indian tourism comprising 40 to 60 percent of all international tourism.

The travel segment includes various travel agencies and tour operators who organize the tours and trips for domestic as well as international visitors. There are various associations that control the activities of travel agents and tour operators. These include:

1. Travel Agents Association of India
2. Pacific Asia Travel Association
3. Travel Agents Federation of India
4. Indian Association of Tour Operators.

Hurdles of Tourism Industry

Socio Political Barrier to Tourism Marketing in South Asia

Tourism is the second largest growing business area after information technology in the global economy. Many of the economies are successful in marketing their country and destinations and generating a substantial amount of foreign exchange from tourism Sector.

Even countries with poor level of infrastructure and facilities are able to attract investors to invest money in their country for tourism promotion. Tourism promotion like other forms of marketing largely depends on the customer traffic.

If there is a growing customer traffic trend then more and more money shall flow to an economy in the form of gross revenue earnings and also as foreign direct investments for tourism destination marketing. The product marketing does not involve much complexity like tourism marketing.

Tourism marketing is a very complex phenomenon because the number of uncontrollable factors is more than the number of marketing mix variables. Though the conventional marketing wisdom says that the larger social and political factors affect the marketing offer in product marketing but it is more prominent in the case of tourism marketing.

The political upspring, terrorism, religious fundamentalism, level of crime perception by the foreign tourist affects the prospects of a destination. The South Asian nations are facing a down turn in the tourism business due to the above reasons.

The factors of low per capita tourist investment sustained effort for tourism marketing by the developing countries have become secondary today. The tourism business is largely governed by the non marketing factors than pure business propositions in South Asia. The geo political developments and the kind of social background has largely affected the perception of the foreign tourists negatively for which the inbound traffic is in a down turn. The decision to establish or maintain a direct investment position abroad necessitates addressing the issue of risk that confronts multinational firms. In the examination of any foreign direct or indirect investment opportunity, the environment encompasses numerous areas of concern for the investing firm.

One of the main functions of risk analysis is to determine when and how economic and non- economic factors can affect the foreign investment climate in a particular country, given that risk is a direct outcome of the political and non-political realities faced by international business. Furthermore, this activity is even more crucial in the current global marketplace, given the increasingly complex and uncertain environmental conditions faced by international tourism promoters, particularly to developing countries.

Socio Political Risk

The business literature speaks about socio political risk in many ways. For example, Weston and Sorge have posited that risk arising from actions of governments or political forces which interfere with or prevent foreign business transactions, or change the terms of agreements, or cause the confiscation of wholly or partially foreign owned business property are called sociopolitical risks. These arise from the uncertainty of social and political events that affect business, rather than with the events themselves. Friedmann and Kim define it as business risk brought by non economic and broad social factors to the business.

A sociopolitical risk event is any outcome in the host country which if it occurs, would have a negative impact on the success of the venture and investment flow. So we can summarize the sociopolitical risk as foreign investors' risk or probability of occurrence of some social and political event (s) that will negatively change the prospect for the profitability of a given investment in the host country. Socio Political Risk and Tourism Promotion Socio-Political risk always plays a negative role to reduce the availability of factors and opportunities of tourism promotion.

Investment in destination promotion, infrastructure development to connect the destination, accommodation facilities, food service, transportation services and retail investments will be discouraged, as the risk of capital loss will tend to rise, primarily because social, political and economic rules governing investments are likely to fluctuate, thereby increasing the uncertainty in the future net return associated with investment projects.

Such increased risks would also raise the cost of capital, as the likelihood of loan defaults would go high and the period of completion of various projects will also rise. Both domestic and international inbound tourism would be discouraged due to such risks. Indeed, capital flight and leakage might be additional outcomes as well.

As sociopolitical risk introduces additional elements of uncertainty into the rules governing tourism investment projects, the risk of capital loss is raised for longer- term projects. Hence, overall productivity in an economy is likely to be lowered via a shift in the marginal efficiency of investment schedule. Sociopolitical risk also negatively influences the timing and pricing of the tourism production process.

For example, the tourism destination planned and promoted with an expected period of launching will not work due to delay in the process of completion of the facilities. So the huge capital invested by intermediaries in promoting destinations in international market will go hay wire due to this problem. The traffic planning of the airlines will also be largely affected by this process. Tourism marketing is a circuitry exercise where multiple sectors are dependant on each other. In a combination they build up a whole tourism product. The increased expectations of changes and uncertainties in the rules of operation of airlines diminish reliability, but they would also produce erratic stops and starts in other tourism investment projects. The economy as a whole would therefore experience a lack of optimal growth path. Thus, it can be argued that political risk increases the uncertainty of the environment in which successful foreign tourism promotion should take place, and hence decrease the incentive to save and invest in tourism by an individual tourist to a particular country destination.

Travel Intermediaries and Tourism Promotion

Travel intermediaries are defined as members in the distribution chain in the tourism marketing channel. They include retail travel agents, tour packagers, incentive marketers, tour wholesalers. They provide lodging, transportation and other travel products and services demanded by domestic and foreign tourists. The ability of travel intermediaries to combine travel products and offer them to customers as a package at a price generally lower than those available to individuals provides travel economy and convenience for a significant segment of tourists.

Travel intermediaries have considerable influence in the decision making process of the tourist. They serve as an opinion leader and expert for taking a travel decision process. They play the role of influencers for many of their loyal customers.

This implies that they are of greater importance to both the tourist and the destination marketer particularly in the cases of destinations with far greater distance from the point of origin. Mclellan and Noe identified them as gatekeepers of information, since they provide information about destinations even if travellers do not choose to use their services. Hawkins and Hudman are of the opinion that the distribution sector of tourism is much stronger and travel intermediaries have far greater power to influence and affect tourist demand when compared to their counterparts in other industries.

The Problem

Despite its variety and immense tourism potential, South Asia's share of the total global tourist arrivals and revenue receipts is meager. This small proportion is concentrated in a few countries particularly India, Nepal and a few parts of Srilanka. One of the most important factors responsible for this poor growth is the phenomenon of sociopolitical risk events.

Since tourism is an extremely fragile industry a crucial consideration in a potential traveller's decision to visit a foreign destination is that country's political stability, social coherence and other real or perceived barriers like service quality, poor infrastructure and health issues. Given the spate of sociopolitical risk events in many counties in South-Asia since the late 1980s, little published research in the tourism literature to date has addressed this problem in any comprehensive manner. The purpose of the study is to examine the effects of touristic attractiveness, channel power and sociopolitical risk on the performance of tourism promotion firms and on travel intermediaries. The two broad purposes of this study are to assess empirically the perceived impact of selected sociopolitical risk variables and to identify other perceived environmental barriers and threats to tourism promotion in South Asia.

Review of Literature

In the tourism literature, few researchers have examined the issue of political risk in South Asian countries and its effects on tourism promotion. Authors have cited sociopolitical risk, lack of investment capital and distance from major tourist- generating markets as barriers to tourism promotions in South-Asia in general. Negative images, lack of foreign exchange for tourism development, lack of skilled manpower, weak institutional frameworks for tourism planning, political instability caused by communal violence, civil war conflicts are inhibitors to tourism development.

However, little is known about how international tourism firms perceive sociopolitical risks and other general barriers and threats to tourism promotion in South Asia.

As stated above, the major source of knowledge upon which this research drew for the delineation of sociopolitical risk factors for tourism is from sociopolitical risk variables existing in general business. The general business literature describes social political risk with illustrations such as civil war, labour conflict, foreign exchange control, production quotas and import-export restrictions. Simon's typology is used for this study.

Methodology

A five point scale with 5 as the most significant negative effect and 1 as very insignificant negative effect was used. The respondents were asked to list different kinds of barriers and threats as they perceive, were of concern to them in doing business in their respective South Asian destinations through a series of open ended questions in the designed instrument. An attempt was made to gain insights into both the qualitative and quantitative aspects of the travel intermediaries' perceptions.

Sampling Procedure and Data Collection

Data for this study were collected between October 2000 and January 2001 which happens to be the main tourist season in various parts of South Asia. Members of Indian Association of Tour operators (IATO) and Indian Association of Travel Agents (IATA) were contacted to supplement the research with a list of clientele of international travel intermediaries operating from various European nations and American states for the survey. These organizations were selected because they provided a membership listing of firms that can be consistently and practically identified as tour operators, destination marketing firms and travel agents whose revenues are derived from packaging and selling tours to South Asian countries.

A sample for the study was drawn using the proportional stratified systematic random sampling method. The sample size was determined to be 230. Of the 230 questionnaires mailed, 27 had undeliverable addresses. After a follow- up, 169 questionnaires were returned, with 129 usable, representing a response rate of 28.6 percent. Although low, such a response rate is typical of mail questionnaire studies that involve business enterprises, in contrast to survey research that involves individuals. The business owners and managers of the organizations selected for the study often face severe time constraints as a result of their work activities and are often inundated with paperwork, meetings and travel making the process to go slow as per their convenience.

Data Analysis

Descriptive statistics were calculated for all variables comprising the scaled sociopolitical risk variables. Factor Analysis through Principal Component Analysis of the seventeen risk variables was conducted to examine the relationship among the interrelated variables. This procedure resulted in two factors. Only factors with eigenvalues greater than 1.0 were included in the final analysis. The extracted factors were rotated using the varimax orthogonal rotation method. A variable was considered to load on a given factor if the factor loading was 0.40 or greater for that factor and less than 0.4 for the other. The reliability of the factors was determined using Cronbach's coefficient alpha test.

The main criterion for inclusion in a particular region is if a respondent indicated sending at least two states or districts in a country then he is included in the region. Those who indicated at least two countries in South Asian region, they were classified into the multiple region categories.

This is done due to the possibility of within country variability in responses to the perceived risk for a country due to the travel intermediary's business link with that country for promoting tourism. The researcher also tried to investigate the relationships between the underlying sociopolitical risk factors and respondents' particular country of tourism promotion in South Asia. Perception towards socio political barriers and threats to tourism promotion is obtained using an open- ended format of the survey instrument.

The researcher conducted content analysis for all open- ended questions in which groupings were made for similar responses into categories and assigning names to the common correlated elements. Content analysis is a research method that uses a set of procedures to make valid inferences from text. The central idea is that many of the words of the text are classified into much fewer content categories. Words, phrases or other units of text classified in the same category are presumed to have similar meanings. This similarity may be based on the precise meaning of the word, or on words sharing similar connotations. This paper has adopted a similar procedure to group several words implying a concern with concept of perceived barriers and threats in South Asia in an attempt to make valid inferences from the open- ended responses.

Blue Print to Success for Indian Tourism Industry

One of the dynamic sectors that contributes significantly to a country's economy is tourism. For many countries such as China, Malaysia and Thailand, tourism contributes as much as 5% of their GDP. The fast pace of technological changes and the interplay among a host of sub-sectors like hospitality and infrastructure make travel and tourism a complex area to study. Moreover, the process of creating a desired image in the minds of potential tourists for a destination involves manipulating both tangible and intangible features associated with a place.

As tourists' lifestyles evolve and expectations expand, marketers of destinations face a difficult task in fulfilling their wishes and aligning the messages with the tourists' lifestyle. Managing the marketing mix effectively in itself is a major task, as interdependence among different elements has to be effectively handled. To top it all, sporadic external events such as outbreak of SARS, attack on WTC and subsequent terrorist attacks cast their shadow.

Variety, they say, is the spice of life. Tourists are always on the lookout for interesting places to visit and absorb the pleasures, luxuries and variety around the world. Attracting first-time tourists and providing service so as to entice repeat visits is naturally the endeavor of different countries.

Besides the traditional tours to natural locales and heritage sites, new segments such as medical tourism and sports tourism are emerging strongly. Cheaper treatment costs in developing countries are drawing patients, who club visits to nearby places of interest post-recuperation. Major sporting events across the world have traditionally attracted sports enthusiasts. Of late, aggressive marketing of sports events is pulling in more and more sports enthusiasts. South Africa, which hosted 2003 Cricket World Cup, attracted 20,000 foreign cricket fans to the country during the event.

Technology is also playing a big role in the changing dynamics of travel and tourism. Internet has enabled worldwide reach for a host of facilitators, and enabled rise of new segments such as FIT (Free Independent Travelers), who shun mass tourism packages and set out to explore on their own.

Internet's absorption by travel and tourism businesses has meant that such travelers can be flexible in their travel plans and arrange for these on the Internet itself. Fewer tourists are opting for prepackaged tours and are arranging themselves travel and accommodation plans through the Internet. This 'dynamic packaging' has been labeled 'the most radical change in the tourism industry in half a century' by The Economist. Jupiter Research estimates that online travel bookings would catapult from $28 billion in 2002 to $53 billion by 2008.

An interesting offshoot of technology for the tourism industry has been the opening of space travel as the last frontier for the obscenely rich. Businessweek, in its February 02, 2004 issue reported, "Getting astronauts and tourists into space on the cheap is the notion behind a privately sponsored race with a $20 million reward. Announced in 1996 by entrepreneur Peter H Diamandis, the X Prize is modelled after the $25,000 Orteig Prize that enticed Charles A Lindbergh to fly solo across the Atlantic in 1927.

To win the X Prize, a privately developed spacecraft capable of carrying three people must soar to 62 miles, then pull-off a repeat within two weeks. That would show the plane's ability to operate like an airliner – and potentially make space travel almost as routine as air travel has become since Lindbergh's feat."

How are marketers positioning their countries so as to reach out to a globally dispersed audience? What challenges are staring at the travel and tourism sector? What are the developments in India? What have been the initiatives and responses of some of the global players in expanding their markets and facing challenges? The book attempts to answer these and other related questions.

Section One – Positioning Destinations

The articles in this section cover the basics of positioning and innovations in marketing of destinations. Travel and tourism is all about journeying to a particular choice of destination. The choice for tourists is so abundant that a good part of one's lifetime would have to be dedicated to cover all the desirable places of visit. Whether one is interested in natural scenic locations, adventure sports, biodiversity, heritage or places of religious importance, there are enough destinations to choose from within the country or overseas.

Countries are increasingly realizing the contribution of tourism to their economies. Many economies are even centred around tourism. Identifying places of interest for potential tourists and creating a positive attitude and perception among them are becoming common practices among national tourism boards. Wide choice for tourists and aggressive marketing by destinations demand a cohesive and focused approach by tourism marketers.

In fact, this is what is leading destination marketers towards devising positioning strategies. For example, Malaysia wants to usurp an Asian experience with its slogan 'Malaysia. Truly Asia.'. India, on the other hand desires to impress with a wide range of experiences, through its campaign 'Incredible India'. Such clear-cut positioning planks demand a good deal of coordination and cooperation among the various stakeholders in the tourism industry.

The first article, "Positioning Tourism Destinations", highlights the importance of taking a proper positioning stance when it comes to marketing of destinations. Hardly, any country enjoys a unique natural competitive advantage, unmatched by other countries in providing a similar experience. Realizing the importance of tourism to their economies, policy makers across countries are putting in place the systems to facilitate growth in tourist arrivals. Tourism marketers are also quite aggressive in promoting different destinations.

While operating in competitive markets, countries need to differentiate their features and offerings in the minds of potential tourists. The image that is cultivated thus must be unique and constantly reinforced.

The author provides guidelines on developing an appropriate positioning plank. These include taking a target audience perspective and combining objective and subjective elements. He also stresses on the need to apply the positioning statement as a guide for maintaining consistency in providing the overall service experience to tourists. It is pointed out that the tests of positioning are to ensure that it should be believable and delivered.

The next article, "Marketing and Destination Growth", discusses the challenges in marketing destinations. While the need to clearly divide the responsibilities between public and private sector agencies is one challenge, managing the interplay among domestic and international elements is another. Moreover, destinations have to be marketed both on the demand side and the supply side. Brand building depends on the nature and extent of relationship among the different stakeholders – National Tourism Offices (NTOs), State Tourism Offices (STOs), Local Government

Authorities (LGAs) and Destination Marketing Organizations (DMOs).

Section Two – Tourism: Challenges

Aspects covered in the four articles of this section are – a blueprint for New Tourism, sustainability of tourism in the 21st century, the state of service quality in Indian tourism and challenges of ecotourism.

Travel and tourism have been transformed over the last few decades globally. More and more destination choices are emerging, options that appeal to a wide cross-section of people are increasing, networking across sectors is on the rise and innovations are the order of the day. In the midst of this transformation, it is time that the industry takes a close look at the challenges facing it.

Aggressive pursuit of tourists and their unrestricted access is putting under strain the ecology of the places where mass tourism prevails. Transport, stay and visit of tourists -- all are contributing to the erosion of nature in its pristine form. A callous attitude towards preserving the ecological balance on the part of tourism boards and irreverence of visitors to the local ecosystem are to be blamed. Aggressive pursuit of short-term numbers in terms of more tourists is preventing a long-term perspective on the sustainability of mass tourism in sensitive places.

Besides the threat to ecosystems, the present state of service quality is another major challenge. Consumers across product categories are getting savvier and more demanding. Service aspects considered as add-ons earlier are taken for granted now. Though tourism is one area where loyalty or repeat visits are relatively less important for marketers, it cannot be ignored that as affluence rises, people tend to visit not only more places but also revisit their favourite destinations. Unsatisfactory service anywhere in the chain (travel, accommodation or food) is likely to create bad publicity, which can have a debilitating affect in a category where word-of-mouth publicity plays a major role.

India has seen a slight jump in international tourist arrivals, up from 2.48 million in 1999 to 2.80 million in 20034. States such as Goa, Rajasthan and Kerala are already well-entrenched as attractive destinations within the country, specially for foreign tourists. Other states such as Maharashtra and Andhra Pradesh are also taking proactive approaches, with the launch of iuxury Deccan Queen rail package by the former and opening of Andhra Pradesh Tourism Information Counter in London by the latter. An opportunity has opened up in the form of NRIs, eager to explore their Indian roots – bringing forth a new segment, Culture Tourism. Even as its global campaign 'Incredible India' promises to change positively the image of the country among international tourists, a great deal needs to be done on the domestic tourism front. As against international standards of 10:1 ratio between domestic and international tourism, India has a corresponding ratio of just 3:1. Opportunity does exist, waiting to be exploited.

The first article in this section, "Blueprint for New Tourism", is a clarion call from The World Travel and Tourism Council (WTTC). The article contends that there is a need for adopting a unified approach on the part of governments and the industry. A new sense of partnership between public authorities and private sector is advocated. New Tourism, according to WTTC, focuses on benefits not only for people who travel, but also for people in the communities they visit, and for their respective natural, social and cultural environment.

Governments must not only coordinate infrastructure development but also guarantee respect for local environments. Industry, on the other hand, must recognize that long-term sustainability of the sector can be ensured by respecting local communities. The article drives home the importance of partnership between public and private sector. Collaborations in developing the human resources and sharing informations are suggested.

"Tourism and Sustainability in the 21st Century", the next article, is sourced from International Friends of Nature. They assert that by shrinking areas of unspoilt nature at destinations, tourism jeopardizes that which it depends on. Thanks to ecotourism, communal management of local resources is under increasing threat. Twenty-first century tourism faces several challenges, such as preserving the nature and culture of destinations; curbing consumption of natural resources; putting in place a professional code of conduct for tour operators and hotels; and devising tourism policies aimed at sustainable destination management.

The next article, "Tourism in India: State of Service Quality", traces the growth in contribution of services sector to India's GDP, discusses the perceptions about customer service and debunks some of the myths associated with customer service in tourism. It is pointed out that when a person moves from being a 'prospect' to a 'tourist', he encounters compromises in service standards.

Some of the myths associated with quality customer service are – having a large workforce translates into better service; training alone takes care of service; being obsequious is what customer service is all about; and providing high salaries ensures better customer service. The author points out that treating employees well and creating satisfied internal customers would help in getting satisfied external customers.

The last article in this section, "Challenges of Ecotourism", discusses the implications of unfettered growth in ecotourism. Author, John N Shores, a consultant, opines that ecotourism has become an all-inclusive term, with multiple definitions abounding. Considering the susceptibility of various ecosystems to the impact of tourism, he advocates a cooperative effort involving travelers, tour operators, local communities and environmentalists to preserve them.

He proposes a six level scale to classify nature-based travel. EL 0, the first level, involves exposing the travelers to and making them aware of the fragility of the ecosystems they visit. EL 1 involves taking monetary support from tourists, to maintain the visited ecosystems. EL 2 is participatory, in that the visitors plant trees or clear litter and make a personal contribution to the preservation efforts.

EL 3 is for certifying that the tour system is benign to the environment. EL 4 is all about demonstrating the net positive effect of travelers, reflected through lower energy consumption and recycling. EL 5 makes the entire system environmentally sound, that encapsulates transport, stay and treatment of residual products.

Section Three – Cases

Over the last two years, global travel and tourism sector has faced multiple challenges in different pockets. Acts of terrorism (9/11 attack on WTO and bomb explosions in Bali, Indonesia) and outbreak of SARS in Far East Asia dampened the spirits to a great extent.

Several airlines had to bear the consequences of reduced air travel, hotels faced drastic reductions in their occupancy rates and tourism-dependent economies experienced a negative growth. Experiences of different players in this sector are compiled in this section. The way the crises were handled by those affected and also the initiatives behind kickstarting growth in tourism, in areas unaffected by the crises, are captured.

The first case, on "United Airlines", discusses its attempt to cope with the dynamic external business environment. Its flexible responses to the severe challenges it faced made its assets more productive. Besides offering convenient scheduling throughout its domestic and international routes, it attracted and retained high-yielding customers.

All airlines operate under the influences of technological, political, social, regulatory and economic forces. By devising a route structure that offered maximum nonstop flights from the Pacific Rim to the US and developing the Star Alliance that brought together 15 carriers, it is in a position to put the days of bankruptcy filing in 2002 behind and emerge out of its problems in 2004.

The next case, "InterContinental Resort Bali", traces the impact of the bomb explosions in Bali, Indonesia and the response shown, in the face of adversity by InterContinental Resort, a premium destination for international tourists. The region enjoys good tourist arrivals from Australia and has a rich history. The InterContinental Resort provides several amenities, such as adventure sports, spa and even a helipad.

The explosions had a devastating short-term impact, with occupancy falling by more than 50 percent. The resort had to shut down half of its blocks and re-deploy employees. The management of the resort swung into action immediately on getting news of the blast and enhanced security for its guests. It had even designed attractive packages to lure domestic tourists. Employees' concerns were also well handled.

SARS (Severe Acute Respiratory Syndrome) ravaged the fortunes of several travel and tourism players in 2003. The case, "SARS – The Industry Responds", is sourced from Deloitte and Touche and captures the effect of the dreaded disease and different responses of regional players in Asia. Many regional airlines had to suspend 50 percent of their flights and hotels saw huge fall in occupancy rates. Government and industry got together in Hong Kong in a campaign called 'We Love HK' to counter the negative impact of SARS. Attractive price-led incentives for travel, hotel stay and shopping were devised and local tourism was promoted in a very big way. Capacity-driven free offers were extended to lure new customers. Employees of Cathay Pacific were given special leave, to avoid job cuts and save money.

"Malaysia – Destination for Business Travellers", the next case focuses on Malaysia's rise as a favourite spot for Meetings, Incentives, Conferences and Exhibition (MICE) travel. The country's share of MICE arrivals tripled between 1999 and 2002. The case analyses this growth and lists out the facilities available; and also highlights the efforts of the country in adding to its strengths. It provides world-class convention centres (upto 35,000 square metres of exhibition space, with some centres having capacity to accommodate as many as 2,000 delegates); hotels adjoining convention centres; customized conference settings; and entertainment options within convention centres. New centres keep cropping up, publicity support is extended by mentioning in the events calendar and familiarization trips for travel organizers are regularly conducted.

Regional cooperation is picking up in travel and tourism sector. The next case, "Regional Networking in Asia", points out how networking is increasing among national tourism organizations in Asia. Impact of SARS seems to have accentuated this development, with international arrivals in Asia dropping by a whopping 80 percent in the immediate aftermath of its detection. Pacific Asia Travel Association (PATA) worked with global media to stimulate travel to the region, as part of its 'Project Phoenix'. Association of South East Asian Nations (ASEAN) set up ASEAN Tourism Fund, to promote the region as a single destination. Tourism Malaysia and Singapore Airlines joined together, to offer a common package tour that covered both Malaysia and Singapore. 'Asia Now' and 'Together in Asia' were the joint promotions undertaken by Hong Kong, Singapore and Thailand in the US and UK respectively.

The next case, "Branding India", is sourced from Swagat magazine and captures the successful efforts of India Tourism Board to reposition India as a premium destination for upscale tourists. As part of the 'Incredible India' campaign executed globally, commercials were released on worldwide television channels, print ads placed in leading travel publications, online banner ads placed on leading portals, newsletters were sent to global travel agents and media meets arranged with travel writers. Thanks to the extensive media coverage, international tourist arrivals picked up significantly and India is able to differentiate itself.

"Branding Kerala", the last case, highlights the success of Kerala in becoming one of the preferred Indian destinations for tourists. A proactive approach of the state administration has resulted in a scenario where tourism has become a major revenue source for the state's economy. Its successful 'God's Own Country' promotional campaign played a major role in the state standing apart from other competing destinations and distinguishing itself. Moreover, popularizing Ayurveda's positive health impact evened out the seasonal trends in tourist arrivals. Its achievement: being named among the ten hot spots for the millennium by Emirates.

Marketing of Tourism Services in India

A Study With Special Reference to Orissa their workers, have contributed a lot in infusing interest to look around to a place for an annual or biannual visit with family members. Even though India has a very meager share amounting to 0.38 percent of tourists and 0.51 percent of the amount of world tourism trade in 2001, it has the hope for attracting more and more foreign tourists by exploiting her unexploited tourist spots of the country. Mostly tourists from North America, Central and South America, Africa, Australia, Western Europe, Eastern Europe, West Asia, South Asia, South East Asia and East Asia are visiting India as foreign tourists.

Out of these the share of North America, Western Europe, West and South Asia occupies a major share in increasing Indian tourism trade. India accounts for four out of five tourists to South Asia. Another healthy trend in the foreign tourism in India since 1991 is the conspicuous increase in business travels with its spin off effects in up-gradation of accommodation and introduction of new technology in communications and other services. On an average, a foreign tourist stays for about 27 days in India which is an important indicator of increase of the foreign exchange earned by the country.

Tourism in India has vast employment potential, much of which still awaits exploitation. At present about 8.5 million persons are directly employed by hospitality services. This is about 2.4 percent of the total work force of the country. In addition, the industry provides indirect employment to about 30 million persons. Further it is interesting to note that the employment generation in proportion to investment is very high in tourism industry. According to an estimate, an investment of Rs.10 lakh creates 89 jobs in hotels and restaurants sector as against 44.7 jobs in agriculture and 12.6 in manufacturing industry.

Another important aspect of employment in tourism is that it employs a large number of women in hotels, airlines services, travel agencies, handicrafts making and marketing and cultural activity centres. As per 1983-84 indices the employment output ratio in tourism was 71, whereas in leather 51, textiles 27, electricity 14, beverages 12 and cement 6.

Generally the visit of a foreign tourist to India provides employment to one person and 6.5 domestic tourists generate one job. Hotel sector is the key segment of tourism industry to earn foreign exchange. Realising the importance of hotel segment the government has taken initiatives to encourage hotel industry by providing tax benefits and other incentives. Foreign investment and collaboration are now facilitated under new economic policy.

The hotel industry has shown a spectacular growth during the last one and half decades. The number of hotel rooms has increased from 30200 in 1986 to 57386 in 1995 and to 62000 in 1996 and to 68000 in 2001. In the approved list of Department of Tourism the classified hotels are 125 in One Star, 286 Two Star, 274 Three Star, 73 Four Star, 56 Five Star, 42 Five Star Deluxe, and 41 of heritage hotel category.

Inspite of rapid strides made by the hotel industry since last one decade or so, the hotel accommodation falls short of the requirement of growing inflow of the tourists. Assuming a modest growth rate of 7 to 8 percent per annum, the requirement to hotel rooms is expected to rise to 91,000 by 2002-03 and to 1.125 lakh rooms by 2005. Besides a large number of budget hotels will be required for about 200 million strong middle class Indian tourists also. Places of tourist interest are so numerous and of varied nature that it is not easy to describe these places comprehensively.

These include mostly the Himalayan Region, the great plain of north India, the peninsular plateau and coastal plains. In general the tourist spots are counted more like Buddhist sites, Shrines, Forts, places of historical importance, hot springs, Jain monasteries, lakes and birds, sanctuaries, religious centres, science spots, sea beaches, summer resorts, water falls and wild lives etc. In this context, a reference can be drawn for Orissa that all above kinds of spots are richly available to attract more and more foreign as well as domestic tourists.

About 25 lakh of domestic tourists and 30000 foreign tourists visit Orissa annually. The share for South Orissa is 30 percent of the total tourist arrival to Orissa. Orissa has several important nationally and internationally famous tourists' centres like Puri, Bhubaneswar, Konark, Cuttack, Chilika Lake, Chandipur, Gopalpur, Beach etc.

The other places are Baripada, Khiching, Baud, Koraput, Bolangir, Jeypore and Udayagiri etc. The area remains unexplored because of want of infrastructural development, more comfortable modes of transport, accommodation etc. Although India has progressed a lot since the fifties with respect to tourism, she is still way behind the developed, even the developing countries. India earns one seventh of China, one fourth of Indonesia and less than half of Philippines from tourism in comparison. The development of tourism depends upon the development of an integrated infrastructure of national and international highways, railways, ports, civil aviation, telecommunication, hotel accommodation and allied services. Inadequacies of such infrastructural facilities adversely affect tourism. The sluggish growth of Indian tourism arises from India's inability to sell effectively her rich tourist potential.

India should market itself as a value added tourism destination stressing its variety and cost effectiveness. Satisfaction of the tourist should be the top priority of the tourist industry. Apart from infrastructural development, tourism requires an environment of peace and stability where the tourist is sure of his safety and security. Political unrest and fear of violence is a death knell to tourist industry. Unfortunately, one part or the other of the country is hit by *bandhs*, strikes, ethnic clashes and insurgency which adversely affect our tourism service marketing. Epidemics, such as plague, AIDS and dengue fever are also detrimental to the growth of tourism.

It is surprising that some small countries like Malaysia, Indonesia, Hongkong and get Singapore have been able to attract more tourists and better receipts than India. Even in terms of quality, the diminutives like Maldives and Bhutan present an appreciable model of sustainable tourism.

In this context, in order to give a philip to the tourism trade the Central Government as well as the State Government should come forward to develop some of the newly unexploited and selected tourist places, diversify some of the culture oriented tourism to holiday and leisure tourism, develop trekking, winter sports, wild life, beach resorts tourism, launching, key markets near tourist centres, provide inexpensive accommodation and to improve service efficiency.

India still hopes better to improve the tourism marketing services and to take an equal and more challenging steps with her competitors in the field more vigoursly.

Promoting Private Sector of Tourism in Jammu and Kashmir

Tourism is considered to be the largest export industry in the world. However, this industry can have an impact on the economy only when it has the motivational force of the Private Sector. Being a service oriented industry it requires professionalism and dedication which are generally lacking in the Public Sector especially in our part of the world.

In the initial stages when tourism was just picking up, the state had to intervene. Private capital would be hesitant in investing without being sure of returns. To give a push to the activity it was essential for the government to go for infrastructure development. A lead was given to the industry and the public sector activities were in fact started totally as part of the department of tourism. It was like facilitating and motivating the private entrepreneurs to take up this activity.

The annual expenditure on maintenance of various establishments run by the government in the shape of huts and tourist bungalows was over Rs.1.50 crores but the total revenue generated was hardly Rs.30 lakhs per year. These establishments were also run as a healthy competition to private sector to keep the prices of these services in check.

The greatest mistake was turning over all these establishments in one go to state run tourism development corporation. In almost all major tourist destinations, the infrastructure for accommodation, food, transport, and recreation is run by the private sector. The government has only to take care of the very basic infrastructure such as road connectivity, power, water, and communications. It has been proved everywhere that any commercial venture run by the government invariably ends in the red.

There are many reasons for this. Firstly, the government service is taken more or less as social security. Employees cannot be fired even if their contribution is zero. The hire and fire system cannot be enforced in government due to a number of reasons. On the contrary in the private sector one has more flexibility both in the selection of the professional staff and policy of hire and fire can be enforced with some minimum guarantees. Apart from tourism, almost all other government corporations are in red. If we have to aim for development of international tourism, we have to promote private sector in a big way. In fact, the state sector organisations should also be gradually disinvested. To begin with some of the lucrative properties should be put up for joint ventures.

Many attempts have been made in the past in this regard but most of these have failed as only loss making properties were offered for joint ventures or outright disinvestment. In addition, the procedures were made so complicated that every enterprising investor got fed up and ran away. The government has to take a conscious decision and plan it properly. Something like a golden handshake has to be worked out for the staff and their consent obtained.

Any ad hoc measure is bound to recoil. These days specialist agencies are available for such jobs. Once it has been sincerely decided that the private sectcr has to be promoted, a number of substantive incentives have to be provided to attract investment. The present incentive rules initiated in mid nineties do not come up to the mark. At the time of declaring these incentives the main motive was to accede to the popular demand of declaring tourism as an industry. This was done with least financial commitment in view of the bad financial position of the state at that time.

Even though tourism was declared to be a priority industry yet the important incentives such as on power were not made available to this sector. It was declared an industry in name only.

The first requirement would be to revise these incentive rules and make investment in tourism related infrastructure most attractive for both local as well as international investors. Not many people know that there are already a host of incentives available as part of the central industrial policy for various tourism projects.

Most of the incentives are for Eco-Tourism projects, which is the most suitable activity for our state having a fragile environment. Lack of knowledge among the members of the trade as well as the administrators is making the local entrepreneurs lose these incentives by default! All tourism ventures should be given a complete tax holiday at least for ten years to motivate the private sector. There should be no bar on the location of these units provided these are in conformity with all local laws. Preference should be given to joint ventures involving local entrepreneurs and also ensuring substantial local employment in such projects. One often hears about single window clearance but it is never implemented on ground.

People coming for investments in any field have to spend months and sometimes years to obtain various clearances. The ideal situation can be setting up of a Tourism Investment Board with private/public sector participation to ensure clearance of projects at an accelerated pace. The areas for investment are extensive. To begin with is the world class accommodation in the major cities like Srinagar and Jammu. Many global hotel chains can be motivated for giving local franchise with government facilitation and if necessary, a counter guarantee in view of the prevailing circumstances.

In fact, totally new resorts can be developed by professional developers and made available for sale among locals who have enough resources for making sizeable investments in this field. Next comes transport. We are nowhere near the minimum world standards. Avis and other rent a car brands which are already in some metros have yet to arrive here. We do not have luxury cars and coaches for sight seeing. Even though over last couple of years locals have taken some initiatives in regard to cars, yet the coaches of the Volvo brand are missing from Kashmir.

There has always been a persistent complaint about lack of recreational and entertainment facilities. We need not always go for night clubs and casinos but there are plenty of other recreational facilities which are missing. These could include bowling alleys, indoor ice and roller skating rinks, amusement parks, cable cars with mountain top panoramic restaurants, theatres, standard art galleries, and museums. There are umpteen other possibilities for decent avenues of entertainment. Unfortunately, instead of promoting private investment, the government is itself venturing into these projects thereby creating some more liabilities for future.

It is the right time for both the industry as well as the government to wake up and prepare jointly a comprehensive tourism policy especially in regard to participation of private sector. The only involvement of the government apart from facilitation and motivation should be monitoring and regulation. We need very strong and upright set ups involving a panel of experts from various related fields of hospitality industry to over see all these developments in regard to tourism. They should adopt international standards and ensure adherence to these by all concerned.

There should also be a fool proof redressal mechanism. It is possible to have these things under the existing legislation in the tourism field by incorporating amendments keeping in view global standards. In addition, various players in the industry need to streamline their own organisations by establishing some sort of ethics committees and setting up reasonable standards of service with continued adherence for allowing membership to these bodies. Defaulters should be automatically thrown out to maintain credibility of standards. Given all the above inputs our motto for future development in tourism should be, "Private Sector, Private Sector, and Only Private Sector"!

2

Agritourism: Innovative Income Generating Activity

Agriculture is backbone of Indian Economy. 85 percent of the population is directly or indirectly dependent on Agriculture where as 26 percent of GDP comes from Agriculture. 110 million farmers are dwelling in 6.25 lakh villages producing more than 200 MT of food grains feeding the country. More than profession, business, agriculture is culture. Hence, adding additional income generating activities to existing Agriculture would certainly increase contribution of Agriculture to national GDP. Serious efforts need to be made in this direction. Agri-Tourism is one such activity.

Tourism is termed as instrument for employment generation, poverty alleviation and sustainable human development. During 1999-2000, direct employment created by tourism is 15.5 millions. Besides, tourism also promotes national integration, international understanding and supports local handicrafts and cultural activities. During 2000, number of foreign tourists visited India is 26.41 lakhs. Indias share in world tour market is just 0.38 percent. With this meager share, foreign exchange earned is Rs.14,475 crores. Turnover in domestic tourism is much more than this. To promote domestic tourism, thrust areas identified by Government of India are development of infrastructure, product development and diversification, development of eco-adventure sports, cultural presentations, providing inexpensive accommodation, streamlining facilitation procedures at airports, human resource development, creating awareness and public participation and facilitation of private sector participation. In this process, important stakeholders are state and central department of tourism, Indian Institute of Tourism and Travel Management, Tourism Development Corporations, foreign embassies, Travel Agents Association of India (TAAI), Indian Association of Tour Operators (IATO), Tourists, Transport Operators Association, Indian convention promotion bureau and Pacific Asia Travel Association (PATA).

Promotion of Agritourism involves some more important stakeholders namely Ministry of Agriculture and line departments at state and central governments and farmers. Promotion of Agri-Tourism needs conceptual convergence with Rural Tourism, Eco-Tourism, Health Tourism, Adventure Tourism and culinary adventures. Greatest advantage of Agri-Tourism are:

1). It brings major primary sector Agriculture closer to major service sector tourism. This convergence is expected to create win-win situation for both the sectors.

2). Tourism sector has potential to enlarge.

3). Agriculture sector has the capacity to absorb expansion in Tourism Sector.

Scope for Agri-Tourism:- Agritourism has great scope in the present context for the following reasons.

(1) An inexpensive gateway:- The cost of food, accommodation, recreation and travel is minimum in Agri-Tourism. This widens the tourist base. Present concept of travel and tourism is limited to urban and rich class which constitute only small portion of the population. However, the concept of Agritourism takes travel and tourism to the larger population, widening the scope of tourism due to its cost effectiveness.

(2) Curiosity about the farming industry and life style:- The urban population basically which has roots in villages always has curiosity about sources of food, plants, animals, raw materials like wood, handicrafts, languages, culture, tradition, dresses and lifestyle. Agritourism which revolves around the farmers, villages and agriculture has the capacity to satisfy the curiosity of this segment of

population. Agritourism provides scope for re-discoursing the rural life which is rich in diversity.

(3) Strong demand for wholesome family oriented recreational activities villages provide recreational opportunities to all age groups i.e. children young, middle and old age, male, female, in total to the whole family at cheaper cost. Rural games, festivals, food, dress and the nature provides variety of entertainment to the whole family.

(4) Health consciousness of urban population and finding solace with nature friendly means Modern lifestyle has made the life stressful and average life span has comedown. Hence, people are in constant search of pro-nature means to make life more peaceful. Ayerveda which is pro-nature medical approach has roots in villages. Indigenous medical knowledge of villagers is respected. Organic foods are in greater demand in urban areas and foreign countries. In total, health conscious urban population is looking towards pro-nature villages for solutions.

(5) Desire for peace and tranquility:- Modern life is the product of diversified thinking and diversified activities. Every individual attempts to work more, in different directions to earn more money to enjoy modern comforts. Hence, peace is always out of his system. Tourism is the means for searching peaceful location. Peace and tranquility are inbuilt in Agritourism as it is away from urban areas and close to nature.

(6) Interest in natural environment - Busy urban population is leaning towards nature. Because, natural environment is always away from busy life. Birds, animals, crops, mountains, water bodies, villages provide totally different atmosphere to urban population in which they can forget their busy urban life.

(7) Disillusionment with over crowded resorts and cities - In resorts and cities, over crowded peace seekers disturb each others peace. Hence, peace is beyond cities and resorts. Even though efforts are made to create village atmosphere in the sub urban areas through resorts, farm houses, it

looks like a donkey painted with tiger colour. Artificiality is highlighted and not satisfying.

(8) Nostalgia for their roots on the farm Cities are growing at the cost of villages. Villagers are migrating to cities in search of jobs and seeking comforts of modern life. Hence, yesterday villagers are todays urbanites. Deep in the heart of urbanites lies the love and respect for their ancestors and villages. Hence, visit to villages satisfies their desire. This is also expressed through the hatredness of urbanites to flat culture and love for farmhouses located in the outskirts of cities. Any opportunity to visit villages and spend time with family is dream of any urbanite. But, minimum decent facilities are always problem. Agritourism attempts to overcome this problem.

(9) Rural recreation Villages provide varieties of recreation to urbanites through festivals and handicrafts. Villagers (farmers) lifestyle, dress, languages, culture / traditions which always add value to the entertainment. Agriculture environment around farmers and the entire production process could create curiosity among urban taught. Places of agriculture importance like highest crop yielding farm, highest animal yielding farm, processing units, farms where innovations tried add attraction to the tourists. Agriculture products like farm gate fresh market, processed foods, organic food could lure the urban tourists. As result of this Agri-atmosphere in the villages, there is scope to develop Agritourism products like Agri-shopping, culinary tourism, pick and own your tree / plot, bed and breakfast, pick and pay, bullock cart riding, camel riding, boating, fishing, herbal walk, rural games and health (Ayurvedic) tourism.

(10) Educational value of Agri-Tourism:- Agri-tourism could create awareness about rural life and knowledge about agriculture science among urban school childrens. It provides a best alternative for school picnics which are urban based. It provides opportunity for hands on experience for urban college students in Agriculture. It is a means for providing training to future farmers. It would

be effectively used as educational and training tool to train agriculture and line department officers. This provides unique opportunity for education through recreation where learning is fun effective and easy.

Basic principles of Agri-Tourism : Agritourism should ensure the following three basic principles.

1. Have something for visitors to see:- Animals, birds, farms and nature are the few things which Agritourism could offer to the tourist to see. Apart from these, culture, dress, festivals and rural games could create enough interest among forest in Agritourism.

2. Have something for visitors to do:- Participating in agricultural operations and swimming, bullock cart riding, camel riding, buffalo riding, cooking and participating in the rural games are the few activities to quote in which tourist can take part and enjoy.
3. Have something for visitors to buy:- Rural crafts, dress materials, farm gate fresh agriculture products, processed foods are the few items which tourist can buy as memento for remembrance.

Three Important Factors which Contribute to the Success of Agri-Tourism

1. Farmer: Majority of the cases, farmer is less educated, less exposed and innocent. For farmer, any outsider is a guest and treated wholeheartedly without any commercial motive. Treating guest is pleasure for them than pain. He entertains the guest while entertaining himself in the process. He is not like an exploitative natured businessman which itself facilitate a clean tourism atmosphere

2. Village : Village, which is located far from the city lacks urban facilities, but blessed with natural resources. The investment is made by nature in the form of water bodies, fields, forest, mountains, deserts and islands. Community is more homogenous and treating a guest is part of their culture rather than a profession leading to natural environment required for urban tourist.

3. Agriculture : Rich resources in agriculture namely land, water and plants are unique from place to place bringing diversity and creating curiosity. Each field is unique which adds to the attraction of tourists. The way of cultivation and the products are great attraction to the urban population. Indigenous knowledge of rural people is a wealth, which adds to novelty and curiosity of urban population.

Combination of farmer, village and agriculture create a wonderful situation which provides unlimited satisfaction to the tourist specially from urban areas.

Agritourism Opportunities in India

Indian tourism industry is growing @10.1%. The World Tourism organization has estimated that the tourism industry is growing at the rate of 4% a year and that by the year 2010 there wil' be more than one billion tourist visit various parts of the world. But Indian tourism industry is growing at the rate of 10% which is 2½ times more that the growth rate at global level. By introducing Agritourism concept, not only present growth rate is sustained but also this value addition contributes to further growth.

India has entered amongest the top 10 tourist destinations list (Conde Nast Travellor A leading European Travel Magazine). India is already established as one of the top tourist destination in the world. Value addition by introducing novel products like Agritourism would only strengthen the competitiveness of Indian tourism industry in global market.

India has diverse culture and geography which provide ample and unlimited scope for the growth of this business. India has diverse Agro-climatic conditions, diverse crops, people, culture, deserts, mountains, coastal systems and islands which provide scope for promotion of all season, multi-location tourism products.

There is an increasing number of tourists preferring non-urban tourist spots (financial express). Hence, there is scope for promotion of non-urban tourist spots in interior villages by establishing Agritourism centres. But, adequate facilities and publicity are must to promote such centres.

Government initiatives and policies in X five year plan, allocation has been increased from 525 crore to 2900 crores. Increased financial allocation reaffirms the government commitment. The increased financial allocation by six times could be used for capacity building of service providers, creation of infrastructure and publicity.

Market mix strategy **:** The proposed market mix strategy for the promotion of Agritourism concept is as follows.

Product - The product in Agritourism is seeing, believing and ultimately experiencing. This experience is unique and unmatched. The experience of climbing a tree , buffalo riding in the pond and enjoying the sugarcane juice in the field itself are unique and none of the million dollar tourist centres can create and offer such experiences.

Price;

a). Customer segment pricing : Domestic and foreign tourist could be priced differently as the capacity to pay is different. For a bullock cart riding, a foreign tourist can pay one dollar where as a domestic tourist can pay only one fourth.

b). Location pricing : Pricing in Agritourism depends upon location and importance. Agritourism which just offers agriculture and rural life as attraction can charge normal pricing. Where as Agritourism spots which are very close to established tourism centres like temple towns, hill stations, around big citres can go far little bit higher charging due to added value. As the pricing in established tourism places are high, it works out to be cheaper for tourist to stay and enjoy in Agritourism spots.

c). Time pricing: Agritourism units can charge higher in peak season i.e. November to January and change less during rest of the period. During rural festivals or at the time of important events Agritourism units can charge more, even though it is during off season.

Place: The place where tourists are accommodated also influence the pricing. It the tourists are accommodated in villages itself with the farmer, the charging can be less where as accommodation in farms cost high. Because, exclusively for tourist purpose infrastructure is created in farm whereas existing facilities are used in farmers house in village.

Promotion: Promotion of Agritourism and strategic alliance can takes place at three levels.

(i) Alliance with airlines, tour operators and foreign embassies. This alliance brings foreign tourists and upper middle class urban tourists into Agritourism fold. It may not be possible for individual farmers to take up this task. Government can assist the Agritourism units through promotion and coordination activities through central and state tourism departments.

(ii) Alliance with hotel industry Large number of domestic tourists can be attracted through alliance with hotel industry. The hotel industry can be used to promote Agritourism concept.

(iii) Promotion by Agritourism units Basically the promotion takes place through mouth to mouth and local publicity given by Agritourism units. As the absorption capacity of each unit is very less, direct marketing with little aggressive mode is enough for a Agritourism units to survive. They can go for combined publicity on cost sharing basis and also publics the Agritourism potential in other part of the country. But, promotion of this group approach needs initial government interventions.

Policies: Some of the policy initiatives of urban government would surely help promotion of Agritourism . They are

(i) Building brand identity Incredible India.

(ii) Rs.60 crore budget for promoting brand

(iii) X five year plan budget increased from Rs. 525 to 2900 crores.

(iv) An allocation of Rs.50 lakhs per village for village tourism has been proposed.

(v) The states are encouraging private public partnership in tourism sector.

Positioning : Ultimately Agritourism concept has to be positioned in the minds of tourists as Come, pluck a fruit, smell a flower, run in the fields, lie on the hay and be lost in rural India.

Entertainment Agritourism : Agritourism involvement in agricultural operations create joyful experience to the tourist. Agri-tourist involvement in milching, harvesting competitions, tree climbing, edible adventure, bullock cart race, buffalo race in wet fields namely Kambala in Karnataka, shooting a coconut target, fishing etc could generate enormous joy atleast cost. There is enough scope to charge entry fee to farmers, providing feed and accommodation on payment basis and charging the participation of Agri-tourist during rural games would also generate income to the farmers.

Some successful entertainment farming enterprises and techniques in Agritourism - International experiences.

Agritourism is a viable income generating activities in many developed counties which would provide lead to promote the same with modifications suiting to our conditions.

They are;

- Wineries with Friday happy hours.
- Arts & Crafts Demonstrations.
- Farm Store : Exhibition of farm equipments
- Roadside Stand selling fresh farm products and craft items
- Processing of farm products and sale
- Demonstration of Agri-activities
- Sheep Shearing.
- Wool Processing.
- Fee fishing / hunting.
- Farm Vacations.
- Bed and Breakfast
- Farm Tours.
- Horseback Riding.
- Cross-country skiing.

- Camping.
- Bad weather - like desert, snow fields, heavy rainfall also attract Agri-tourists
- Picnic Grounds.
- A shady spot for visitors to rest like a big baniyan tree
- Educational Tours for school children, officers and progressive farmers
- Farm Schools to teach a particular skill
- Outdoor Schools which are mobile in nature teaching agriculture
- Herb Walks.
- Workshops on interesting, emerging agriculture topics
- Festivals with wide publicity and sponsorship
- Cooking Demos to satisfy housewives.
- Pick-Your-own Pumpkin Patch.
- Rent an apple tree.
- Moonlight activities.
- Pageants.
- Speakers who can attract Agro-tourist narrating Agricultural experiences.
- Regional Themes like tribal coffee of Kerala, Andaman spices etc
- Crop Art.
- Pizza Farm.
- Historical Recreations like highlighting a oldest farm etc.
- Log Buildings.
- Antique Villages.
- Collection of old farm Machinery.
- Miniature Village.
- Farm Theme Playground for Children.
- Fantasyland.

- Gift Shop.
- Antiques.
- Crafts.
- Crafts Demonstrations.
- Food Sales.
- Lunch Counter.
- Cold Drinks.
- Restaurant.
- Theme (apple town, etc.).

The issues which needs attention for the promotion of Agritourism are :

1. *Publicity:* It is difficult to provide publicity to a remote Agritourism unit. Hence, either collectively such Agritourism operators can provide publicity or organizations like ITDC, State tourism development corporations, NGOs, press and tour operators can take up this responsibility Information technology can play very important role in promotion of Agritourism. An interactive website containing all details about Agritourism locations and a toll free 24 hours help line can provide necessary information to Agri-tourists.
2. *Transport :* Reaching the remote Agritourism units is the greatest challenge due to lack of approach roads and poor transportation facilities in rural areas. Tele connectivity is must which is yet to reach villages. Government should play important role in creating these facilities namely roads, transport and telecommunication to rural areas specially where Agritourism units are established on priority basis. This efforts could be effective with private participation in partnership mode.
3. *Accommodation:* Safe and clean accommodation is must in Agritourism. Urban and foreign tourists look for these minimum facilities. Orienting Agri tour operators on one hand and providing incentive to such efforts on other hand is necessary. Regular clean water supply and neat

toilets are important. At the same time, it is necessary to limit modern facilities in which Agri-tourist is not interested.

4. *Networking:* Networking public and private stakeholders at national and state level to assist the Agritourism operator at remote place is necessary. This network can get policy support, infrastructure and publicity to Agritourism units.
5. *Capacity building of farmers:* Farmer need to be oriented on maintenance of facilities, hospitality and public relation which he is not aware.
6. *Safety of tourists:* Agritourism units are located in remote areas which lacks roads, medical facilities, telecommunication and sometimes threat from theft and wild animals. Hence, support of local population is must besides facilities for emergency medical care.
7. *Private:* pubic partnership Agripreneurs, farmers organizations, co-operatives, NGOs and agribusiness companies can take up these ventures with the help of farmers and government agencies tour operators. Transporters and hospitality industry would also benefit in the process.

Agritourism Growing in India

The Agri Tourism Development Corporation (ATDC) is keen on tapping the Rs 4,300-crore agri tourism industry by expanding its reach across India, starting with Maharashtra .

ATDC last year had launched a pilot project at Malegoan spread over 100 acres, which had over 7,000 tourists, resulting in a 25 percent increase in the annual income of farmers.

ATDC will now repeat the Malegoan model with 25 projects across Maharashtra and is also exploring the possibilities in Punjab and Andhra Pradesh.

The corporation has also roped in Bank of India and Syndicate Bank for financing of the projects.

"By April 2007, we will be ready to start the tours and build the capacities required in Maharashtra," said Pandurang Taware, director (sales and marketing), ATDC, the nodal agency helping farmers market their farms and also providing training to them for starting agritourism units on a 20-22 percent revenue-sharing basis.

The Malegoan unit comes under the Agriculture Development Trust and will be used as a base platform for training and experimentation by ATDC.

Farmers can find an additional source of income from agriculture, considering the fact that over 70 percent of the urban population has grown up without seeing a village.

"Agri tourism is a Rs 4,300-crore industry and is an effective means of creating employment opportunities. For every job created, there are 11 indirect jobs," said Rajendra Pawar, chairman and managing director, Agriculture Development Trust.

ATDC has upcoming projects in Rihe village near Hinjewadi, Junnar, Sangamner, Rajgurunagar and is also asking farmers, trusts or villages to submit information like their historical background, proximity to any scenic places like temples, forts, dams, etc. On the basis of this information, ATDC will prepare a feasibility report.

The feasibility report will act as the base document for sanctioning of loans from banks. "We will also be the guarantors for the project," said Taware, adding that projects require minimum finances for providing accommodation for one person per acre and toilets.

The Malegoan Agri Unit saw farmers continue with their normal farming activities from Monday to Friday and conduct agri tours as an additional business activity on the weekends - Friday to Sunday.

The farmers also provided the guests with food and entertainment programmes besides giving them an opportunity to participate in the farming activities.

Ecotourism Tourism Development in India

To be with nature and enjoy its creations in the most natural way without endangering it is known as ecotourism. It can take several forms: to be in a beautiful natural forest or landscape; to enjoy watching animals, birds and trees or corals and marine life in a sea; to engage in trekking, boating or rafting; and to wander into sand dunes.

These are some of the common forms of ecotourism. Though the word ecotourism has gained importance only recently, India has been experiencing it through the ages.

Geographical Diversity of India

India is a country of continental dimensions consisting of four distinct regions, namely, the great mountain zone, plains of the Ganga and the Indus rivers, the desert region and the southern peninsula. Almost two-thirds of the Himalaya is in the mountain zone of India, including large plateaus and valleys. The plains of the Ganga and the

Indus are formed by basins of three distinct river systems, the Indus, the Ganga and the Brahmaputra. The desert region consists of the great desert and the little desert. The great desert extends from the Rann of Kachchh and runs through the Rajasthan-Sind frontier. The little desert extends from the Luni River between Jaisalmer and Jodhpur up

to the northern wastes. The peninsular plateau is flanked on one side by the Eastern Ghats and on the other by the Western Ghats. Between the Western Ghats and the Arabian Sea there is a narrow coastal strip, while between the Eastern Ghats and the Bay of Bengal lies a broader coastal area. India is thus endowed with every land form, mountains, plains, deserts and sea coasts.

Ecotourism Resources

The geographical diversity of India has also given it a wealth of ecosystems which are being protected and preserved. They have also become the major resources for ecotourism. One specific element is biosphere reserves.

These are multipurpose areas protected in order to preserve the genetic diversity and integrity of plants, animals and microorganisms in representive ecosystems. There are seven such reserves in India at present:

Nilgiri; Nanda Devi; Nokrek; Great Nicobar; Gulf of Mannar; Manas and Sunderbans. A second element is mangroves, which are specialized forest ecosystems in tropical and sub-tropical regions of the world bordering sheltered sea coasts and estuaries. Major mangrove areas are: Northern Andaman and Nicobar; Sunderbans; Bhitarkanika and Mahanadi Delta; Coringa, Godavari Delta and Krishna Estuary; Pichavaram and Point Calimar; Goa; Gulf of Kutch; Coondapur; Achra/Ratnagiri; and Vembanad.

The third element is coral and coral reefs. There are four coral areas identified in India so far: Gulf of Mannar; Andaman and Nicobar Islands; Lakshadweep Islands; and Gulf of Kutch.

The fourth element is the great and little deserts in the North-Western region of the country. This is a distinct ecosystem which has attracted the fascination of tourists.

The fifth element consists of mountain and forests, including great Himalayas and other mountain ranges in the country. Along with their forests, rivers and snow, they have also become great attractions for eco-tourists.

The country has an area of about 752 million hectares designated as forests, and of which about 406 million hectares are classified as reserve forests and 215 million hectares as protected forests.

India's sixth element is the flora and fauna which are very abundant. There are about 45,000 species of plants, including shrubs. The country also has a great variety of fauna, numbering a little over 65,000 knownspecies, including 1,228 species of birds, 428 species of reptiles, 372 species of mammals, 204 species of amphibians and 2,546 species of fishes.

In order to protect and preserve these genetic resources, India has created 75 national parks and 421 wildlife sanctuaries in different parts of the country.

Some have already become popular with tourists, such as Kaziranga and Manas in Assam; Jim Corbett Park in Uttar Pradesh; Bharatpur, Ranthambore and Sariska in Rajasthan; Kanha and Bandhavgarh in Madhya Pradesh; Bandipur in Karnataka; and Simlipal in Orissa.

Development of Ecotourism

India has consistently included environmental and ecological safeguards in the development of ecotourism in order to avoid gross commercialism. Opening ecological areas for tourism is generally done after careful assessment of carrying capacity to ensure that nature's bounty is not destroyed. India has also always tried to ensure that tourism does not impinge on the culture and heritage.

In general, a sound and sensitive environmental approach is adopted to tourism development planning and is integrated with other activities to ensure the following:

a) Levels of development are to be compatible with the general capacity of the physical environment and resources.

b) Sufficient facilities and services need to be provided to serve tourists and the local population.

c) Hotel rooms must be distributed in such a manner that the natural characteristics and qualities of the area are enhanced.

d) The three dimensional manifestation of tourism development should be designed carefully and with a sensitivity that merges with the surroundings and enhances the natural beauty.

e) Architectural heritage sites and other areas of historic value are to be adequately protected.

In the initial years of ecotourism development, greater emphasis was given to the development of tourism in the Himalayas and the deserts. One of the earliest projects was the Gulmarg Winter Sports Resort. However, the focus has been on the provision of basic minimum facilities for visits by eco-friendly tourists to the hills, national parks and wildlife sanctuaries. Forest lodges and viewing towers were provided in some of the important sanctuaries along with transport facilities in the form of jeeps and elephants.

There are several interesting trek routes of varying difficulty in the Himalayas. Facilities like camping sites, trekkers' huts, tents and trekking equipment are provided to encourage the development of a few of these routes and promote trekking tourism. Several bodies of water including lakes, back waters and seas constitute major sources of tourist attractions.

Facilities like houseboats, water sports equipment, glass bottom boats, hovercraft, etc. are provided to benefit tourists.

Landscaping and upgrading the environment of parks, gardens and other natural areas has been another stream of developmental activity associated with ecotourism. Creation of public conveniences and road side amenities was also given considerable importance in the development process.

Some recent initiatives in the development of ecotourism include the establishment of a resort in 1988 with 70 beds at Bangaram Island in Lakshadeep with private sector participation. The crystal clear sea water, abundant marine life and corals provide an ideal setting for enjoying nature's beauty.

The Coconut Grove at Kumarakam and Spice Village at Thekady in Kerala are some new additions to India's ecotourism resorts. These are private enterprises which specialize in providing experiences with nature in fullmeasure.

India has also been aware of the importance of preparing master plans for the sustainable development of tourism.

A study on the sustainable development of tourism at Andaman and Nicobar Islands is now underway with the assistance of UNDP and WTO. Similar studies are also being considered in other areas identified for resort development.

Himalayan Tourism Advisory Board

The Himalayan Tourism Advisory Board (HIMTAB) was set up in 1987 as a voluntary consultative mechanism for cooperation among the states to promote Himalayan tourism. The Board meets at different places in the Himalayan states to formulate policies and programmes for the development of tourism in the region. Issues already considered by the Board in various meetings include development of alternative resorts to reduce over-crowding in the established tourist spots, use of alternative sources of energy, registration of porters and guides, coordination of mountain rescue operations, preservation of ecosystems, establishment of effective communication, garbage disposal systems and safety and security of tourists.

Publicity and Promotion of Ecotourism

As a major segment of Indian tourism, ecotourism is given considerable importance in publicity and promotion. The places being developed for ecotourism are given publicity through print and electronic media. A brochure listing some simple codes to follow in order to become an eco-friendly tourist has been publishied recently by the Department of Tourism.

Controls and Sustainability

India has legislation to protect untouched ecologies and sensitive ecosystems. Some important laws are the three following:

(a) The Forest (Conservation) Act, 1980 controls the use of forests for non-forestry uses.

(b) The Wildilife (Protection) Act, 1972 designates the national parks and wild life sanctuaries and stipulates a comprehensive framework for wildlife protection and conservation.

(c) The Environment Protection Act, 1986 stipulates several measures for protecting and improving the quality of the environment and preventing, controlling and abating environmental pollution. Coastal Regulation Zones (CRI) were gazetted by a notification under the Act in 1991 and a wide range of activities have been prohibited within 500 metres of the high tide line.

In addition, the Department of Tourism has been developing a national policy and guidelines for the development of tourism in forests, deserts and marine systems. Once formulated, these guidelines would be implemented to ensure the sustainability of ecotourism development.

Ecotourism-prospects and Problems

Ecotourism the fastest growing segment of International tourism scene urgently needs proper guidelines & directions of international standards to sustain its natural growth. In each country many products are developed without any general standards, to suit their own interest. This will lead into major problems in the future. As ecolabeling is becoming a very important marketing tool in selling of tourism products all over the world, a conscientious effort from all the concerned in developing management and marketing of ecotourism products is the need of the hour. The ecotourism products should be diverse as each country has its own needs and requirements, but it should have a pattern.

The various standards introduced by numerous organisations in conceptualising, developing and sustainably managing and marketing ecotourism products should have a common direction. The chances of ecotourism practitioners all over the world over to come together and interact together to solve their management problems should be made frequently and more effectively through various organisations. It should be planned regionwise, countrywise as well as globally, both at micro level and macro level during these interactions. The numerous problems arising during the ecotourism development and management should be brought to the notice of all the concerned and serious discussion and interactions followed, will be of great help to all. The experiences at micro level lead to answers to the questions of macro level.

Ecotourism as the Future of Modern Day Tourism

As the future of tourism depends on sustainability ecotourism has all the prospects to become very popular among the travelers. Mass tourism and tourism in general damages the mother nature in many ways. More travellers in future will opt for ecotourism. An awareness should be created among the travelers in opting a tour, which is sustaining mother nature, supporting local community, their culture, traditional ways of life and not exploiting them in any way. Only then the damages created by mass tourism should be reversed.

The ultimate aim of tourism should be while attaining mental and physical happiness by experiencing varied environments, way of life style, cuisine, culture etc without causing much damages to the visiting population and contributing to the economic, mental, physical characteristic of them. Thus ecotourism will benefit both the visitors as well as the host community. Thus ecotourism should be the role model in popularizing the responsible tourism and fair trade in tourism. Ecotourism should help the visitors for a learning experience of a diverse environment, ambience causing minimum damages to mother nature and its various components.

Need Versus Greed

Like all business activity, tourism is centred around economics, more money with less expenses. But careful strategies are essential to control the needs of the people than their greeds. Once measures are taken to look after the needs, then sustainability could be attained. On the other hand, if the greed of the people became prominent, the end result will be disastrous like killing a goose laying golden eggs. Thus ecotourism practitioners all over the world has to come together and evolve a methodology, look after the needs and not greeds for the sustainance of themselves as well as mother nature.

Ecotourism as a Philosophy and Way of Life

Practitioners of serious ecotourism has to develop a separate mind set other than normal tourism professionals as ecotourism is a way of life in itself. A serious ecotourism practitioner has to look into the possibilities of always choosing for the right things. Their practice has to be routine for day to day life conducting of business in a ecotourism resort.

They are the honorary emissaries to function as a role model for the sustainable ecotourism practices. They should also try their best to promote the philosophy to all others. Thus preaching and practice should go together. Successful ecotourism practitioners are always not prophets of doom, but are glittering rays of hope for the betterment humanity as well as mother nature.

As tourism is becoming the biggest economic activity in the world in the 21st century, ecotourism practices and principles has more relevance than ever. Let us hope by working together, we could hope for a better world where all are equally important.

Biographical Note

Babu Varghese, aged 51 years presently the Managing Director of Tour India with almost 30 years of experience in the field of tourism in the southern state of India called Kerala. With a Masters Degree in Zoology and M.Phil in Behavioural Science, started Tour India as a tourists guidance bureau way back in early seventies, when tourism was only emerging as a business. In the course of many years learned the needs of the tourism industry by introducing Kettuvallam Houseboats for comfortable cruise in canals, converting the traditional cargo boats. Thus saving the traditional boats and offering a livelihood for the boat men and adding a new tourism product for Kerala. After the runaway success of Kettuvallam Houseboats, introduced Tree Houses in the Green Magic Nature Resort for serious ecotourists using local men, materials and indigenous techniques in northern Kerala. The Treehouse and Ecolodges has won many international prizes including the DRV from Germany for Tourism and Environment in 1998.

Later introduced modified Bullock-carts for rural and ethnic tours and Marine Sports Fishing at Kovalam for the anglers around the world. Presently involved in marketing the "Periyar Tiger Trail" - a protection oriented adventurous trekking programme involving the former poachers. Conservation will have double effect when the former poachers are entrusted the job of protectors. The nature is protected and growing back its lost glory as poachers are not poaching. The negative dependency of the poachers are made into positive dependency as they are helping to arrest other poachers, while attempting to poach.

Resources of Tourism Growth is Tourism an Economic Activity to Pursue?

The success of your tourism program depends on strong consensus among residents to pursue tourism development. Seasonal population fluctuations will affect community organizations and services; and therefore, tourism development may alter the lives of many residents. The goals of tourism development need to be integrated with your community goals.

Tourism development will expand the economic base. It can provide new jobs and economic stability. Tourism will also help to diversify your economy not only to industries that directly meet the needs of potential tourists but also in bringing new community services to permanent residents. At the same time, tourism development may create several problems in the county. It is important to have an understanding of challenges and opportunities of tourism development, following overview is intended to provide you with some background:

Tourism Development for Rural Communities

At the start of the new millennium, tourism is firmly established as the number one industry in many countries and the fastest growing economic sector in terms of foreign exchange earnings and job creation. International tourism is the world's largest export earner and an important factor in the balance of payments of most nations. In the United States, tourism is the nation's second largest retail industry. In Illinois, total tourism travel expenditures in 1990 were approximately $14 billion. In addition, $2 billion in taxes were generated and another $3.4 billion were realized in payroll receipts. Almost 250,000 people are employed in travel related industry. Projections for the state suggest growth in the tourism industry have flattened over the past few years but the state still retains its position as a tourism leader in the Midwest.

Tourism revenues are not evenly distributed across Illinois. Studies show that the Chicago area accounts for the majority (over 70%) of all tourism dollars entering the state, while other large cities in downstate Illinois account for a large percent of the remaining share of the state's tourism income. Much of the disparity in tourism revenues throughout Illinois can be explained by two important facts. First, over 50 percent of all pleasure travel in the United States is oriented toward visiting family and friends; because of this, population centres will always attract the majority of tourists. Second, large cities have the economic base (i.e., infrastructure) with which to effectively absorb tourists' expenditures.

Rural communities considering tourism as part of their economic base face some important and exciting challenges. Not every community is suited for tourism development, nor is tourism appropriate for every community. However, tourism development in a rural community touches almost everyone.

From a positive side, tourists tend to purchase products from a variety of sources— from hotels, motels, Bed and Breakfast Inn's (B&Bs), restaurants, gas stations, grocery stores, craft stores, bait shops, and recreational facilities. The jobs tied to these businesses generally do not require extensive training or skills. These businesses may be major employers of high school students and senior citizens.

Tourism also provides the basis upon which communities can renew their pride in heritage and the quality of life; traditional crafts, ethnic cultures, historic rites and celebrations are a few examples of "attractions" which are increasingly popular among tourists. Conversely, tourism tends to be highly seasonal, cause disruptions in community traffic flows and may attract certain elements of society which conflict with the values of the community. The challenge, then, it is to encourage (i.e., develop) those elements which you believe provide the basis for an acceptable level and theme of tourism development while minimizing those aspects which conflict with the values of community life.

Tourism as an Activity

Tourism is traditionally referred to as an industry which comprises attractions, restaurants, accommodations and transportation. However, the tourism industry also includes the local newspaper, grocery stores, card shops, hardware stores and bakeries —essentially all of the stores which make up the economic base of the community. Thus, while the industry often appears to be dominated by giants like Holiday Inn Corporation, Hilton, United Airlines and McDonalds, most tourism industry operators (98%) are small "mom and pop" businesses.

Today, professionals involved in tourism development focus on tourism as an activity engaged in by people who travel. This activity includes everything from those activities dealing with the planning of the trip, travel throughout the trip, actual "visit" to attractions, as well as memories about the trip. This view of tourism as an activity focuses attention on the reasons why people travel, the activities in which they participate and the role of tourism businesses in facilitating this activity.

The most important reason for travel to Illinois is to visit family and friends, according to recent studies (Fesenmaier, D., 1992, 1993) . These studies show that the need to be with people, to give and receive love, is the driving force for much tourism travel. The activity of tourism, then, enables a couple, a family, or even unacquainted groups to create or manipulate settings with which to satisfy this need for companionship. These studies also show that tourism is an activity which enables people to relax, to exercise, to learn about oneself as well as the world we live in and to gain social recognition. The reasons for pleasure travel tend to be mixed and changing. The needs of companionship, exercise and learning might provide the basis for one trip, while social recognition provides the basis for another trip.

Motivation for Travel

Relaxation: Escape, sand and sun, dropping out, tension reduction, exercise.

Belonging: Visit family and friends, companionship, searching for roots.

Knowledge: Culture, wanderlust, education programs.

Status: Ego-enhancement, social recognition, status and prestige.

Security: Health, active recreation.

Aesthetics: Environment, scenery.

Source: Mill, R.C and Morrison A. The Tourism System: An Introductory Text, Prentice Hall, 1992 Second Edition.

From this perspective, the tourism industry becomes the facilitator, the setting for tourists to meet their needs. Tourist attractions such as Disney World, for example, provide the basis for families to be together, for people to identify with "being young," for others to relax and drop out. Other persons might visit for the "excitement" and stimulation of a parade or a ride through

Space Mountain. The success of such an attraction is tied to its ability to recognize travelers needs and to provide the settings where their needs can be addressed. In essence, Disney World is an attraction where visitors are encouraged to "create" those experiences which meet their needs.

The Challenge for Tourism Development

Rural America, represented by a unique combination of physical, social and cultural characteristics has been the focus of a number of important studies in recent years. These studies have identified a variety of major events that have adversely effected the economy of rural America. These include the "energy crisis" of the early 1970s, two major recessions, high inflation, the decline in U.S. competitive edge in world markets and large federal and state budget deficits. These events have affected the nation's economy to such an extent that in rural communities agriculture no longer plays the dominant role it did 30 years ago. Studies have shown, however, that rural communities possess a large aggregate of untapped assets which offer substantial opportunity for development.

Travel to rural areas accounts for about one-third of all pleasure trips. The typical rural tourist travels an average 680 miles from home, takes a trip that lasts an average of 4.6 nights, stays with friends or relatives, makes his/her own arrangements, is accompanied by at least one other member of the same household, is married, has at least a high school diploma, owns his/her own home and maintains a full-time job.

Because of the continued increase in the demand for leisure travel in the United States, it is believed that rural America will be a prime beneficiary of this increase in tourism travel.

These trends suggest a substantial change in the nature of tourism travel in United States. They show that tourists will support American heritage and culture and increasingly will be willing to "pay the price" for high quality leisure experiences. The tourism industry will change dramatically to provide these personalized experiences and services. These trends focus attentions on the resources of rural communities: culture, values, quality environment and a "friendly" lifestyle. For rural communities wanting to invest time, energy and money in tourism, the challenges are substantial. But, given the trends in society identified above, appear to offer great opportunity to create a vital and sustainable industry. Community involvement is a basic requirement for a successful tourism program. Planning by business leaders and community leaders is critical to establishing acceptable tourism development strategies. Recognizing that the tourism industry within a community provides for and facilitates tourists' experiences, the second challenge is to identify and evaluate all aspects of the industry within the context of these experiences.

Training in Tourism Sector

Delimitation of the Hotel, Catering and Tourism (HCT) Sector

When the ILO Governing Body created the ILO Industrial Committee for the Hotel, Restaurant and Tourism Sector, which subsequently became the Committee for the Hotel, Catering and Tourism Sector, the sector included:

(a) hotels, boarding houses, motels, tourist camps, holiday centres;

(b) restaurants, bars, cafeterias, snack bars, pubs, night clubs, and other similar establishments;

(c) establishments ... for the provision of meals and refreshments within the framework of industrial and institutional catering (for hospitals, factory and office canteens, schools, aircraft, ships, etc.);

(d) travel agencies and tourist guides, tourism information offices;

(e) conference and exhibition centres.

Statistics are being organized according to the International Standard Industrial Classification of all Economic Activities (ISIC), the latest edition of which is ISIC Rev. 3. In that classification, the sectors most relevant for the ILO definition of the sector are Hotels and restaurants (division 55) 2 and Activities of travel agencies and tour operators, Tourist assistance activities (class 6304). Other organizations concerned with tourism, including governments, intergovernmental organizations and NGOs, often use much broader definitions of the term than that used by the ILO. They subsume under it all services and products consumed by tourists, including transport. In the ILO denomination of the sector, the part referring to "tourism" only covers travel agencies and tour operators.

Tourism Satellite Accounts

As an economic concept, tourism is defined in "demand side" terms, as it comprises all services and goods consumed by tourists as well as all investments made to satisfy that consumption. A tourist has been defined by the United Nations as a traveller or visitor.

The credibility and international comparability of "tourism statistics" depend heavily on: (1) a consensus regarding the choice of "tourism characteristic industries", i.e. those industries on which tourism demand has the most important direct impact, and an estimation of the "tourism ratio" of their output; as well as (2) the methods used to calculate the indirect effects on the output of many other industries.

Statistical presentations differ in whether they include such indirect or induced effects in the measurement of tourism in the economy. Probably the most inclusive choice of industries is the one adopted by the World Travel and Tourism Council (WTTC), a private organization. It takes into account industries whose "tourism ratio" is low but whose products and services represent high value, such as the construction and operation of transport infrastructure.

The demand side nature of tourism is the basis of a methodology for Tourism Satellite Accounts (TSAs) developed by the World Tourism Organization and OECD and adopted by the United Nations Statistical Commission early in 2000. The ILO has been cooperating with those organizations in accordance with the mandate given to it by the Tripartite Meeting on the Effects of New Technologies on Employment and Working Conditions in the Hotel, Catering and Tourism Sector in 1997, with a view to providing a methodology for the production and presentation of tourism-relevant labour statistics to supplement the TSAs. A proposal has been formulated by the ILO for a tourism labour accounting system (TLAS) within that framework, 8 based on its work on a general labour accounting system. A detailed "employment module" presenting labour-related issues was already attached to the TSA by the OECD, but this module does not provide the necessary framework for linking the different units, variables and classifications used when collecting labour statistics from many different sources.

Some early efforts towards TSA presentations have already been made by a number of pioneer OECD countries on the basis of figures from national accounts systems as required in the methodology adopted by the United Nations Statistical Commission in 2000. The World Travel and Tourism Council (WTTC) has been producing Tourism Satellite Accounts using a simulation method and based on a non-systematic variety of statistical sources.

Tourism Economy

The contribution of tourism activities to national GDPs, direct and indirect, varies by country and region as illustrated by the WTTC's estimates .

The Caribbean is the most tourism oriented region in the world. It is estimated that in 2000, tourism employed 3.1 million people either directly or indirectly, thus accounting for 13.4 percent of total employment. Direct employment in the tourism characteristic industries alone amounts to 5 percent of total employment. Visitor expenditures contributed an estimated US$17 billion, or 18.4 percent, to export revenues. Countries whose international tourism receipts exceed 5 percent of GDP or 10 percent of export revenues are considered to be "tourism countries" for the purposes of the World Trade Organization.

Tourism is expanding in almost all countries including the developing countries. In fact, mass tourism involving domestic and regional travel is becoming an important phenomenon in several developing countries of Asia, Latin America, the Middle East and Africa, where the proportion of the population actively participating in domestic and regional tourism is predicted to grow considerably. In particular, regional tourism originating from China is expected to change the Asian tourism industry profoundly within the next one to two decades.

Importance of International Tourism

Tourism across national borders represents a variable but generally large proportion of total tourism. Especially in a number of developing countries a significant proportion of gross domestic product is generated by activities designed to satisfy international tourism, which thus represents an important export activity in many countries. Globally, the World Tourism Organization (WTO) predicts that the number of international tourists will reach almost 1.6 billion by the year 2020 (as opposed to 565 million in 1995), and that international tourism receipts will exceed US$2,000 billion. The estimated growth of world international tourism arrivals of 4.5 percent perannum will pose enormous challenges and opportunities for those regions and countries seeking to benefit from tourism while avoiding its negative impacts.

The top ten tourism destinations in the world in terms of tourism receipts are the United States, Spain, France, Italy, United Kingdom, Germany, China, Austria, Canada and Greece. The United States earns the most from tourism, with total tourism revenues of US$74.4 billion in 1999, followed by Spain and France. Even though tourism is a global industry, the majority of receipts still accrue to the Americas and Europe, reflecting both the fact that closeness to origin of the travellers still matters and the fact that countries in these regions have had the time, resources and demand needed to develop their tourism industries.

For many countries, international tourism is an indispensable source of foreign currency earnings. According to the World Tourism Organization, tourism is one of the top five export categories for 83 percent of countries and the main source of foreign currency for at least 38 percent of them. In 1998, international tourism and international fare receipts (receipts related to passenger transport of residents of other countries) accounted for roughly 8 percent of total export earnings from goods and services worldwide. Total international tourism receipts, including those generated by international fares, amounted to an estimated US$532 billion, surpassing all other international trade categories.

As a by-product of the rapid fall in the real costs of long-distance travel, the developing regions of the world participate fully in the worldwide growth of international tourism. However, market shares vary strongly from one county to another and within very short periods, reflecting the economic or security crises affecting different countries or regions.

A Changing Tourism Industry

Mass tourism in and from the industrialized countries is a product of the late 1960s and early 1970s. Since then a number of interrelated developments in the world economy, such as overall economic growth and various other socioeconomic changes, government policies, technological revolution, changes in production processes and new management practices, have converted part of the industry from mass tourism to so-called "new tourism". The latter connotes the idea of responsible, green, soft, alternative and sustainable tourism, and basically refers to the diversification of the tourism industry and its development in targeted, niche markets. Competition in the new tourism is increasingly based on diversification, market segmentation and diagonal integration.

The identification and exploitation of niche markets has also proven to be a great source of revenue within new tourism, suggesting that further diversification and customization can be expected in the years to come. Market segmentation – as exemplified by ecotourism, cultural tourism, cruise and adventure tourism – is clearly in evidence and is experiencing great success. New niche markets are constantly being identified in an attempt to diversify the industry further. Customization has also begun to play an important role in the industry. Tourism players are attempting to gain a competitive edge by catering for the individual needs of clients. The tourism product has thus been transformed over time from being completely dominated by mass tourism to an industry that is quite diversified and caters more to the individual needs of its participants.

Changing Consumer Preferences

Today, new consumers are influencing the pace and direction of underlying changes in the industry. The "new tourists" are more experienced travellers. Changes in consumer behaviour and values provide the fundamental driving force for the new tourism. The increased travel experience, flexibility and independent nature of the new tourists are generating demand for better quality, more value for money and greater flexibility in the travel experience.

The new consumers also reflect demographic changes – the population is ageing, household size is decreasing and households have greater disposable income.

Changing lifestyles of the new tourists are creating demand for more targeted and customized holidays. A number of lifestyle segments – families, single parent households, "empty nesters" (i.e. couples whose children have left home), doubleincome couples without children – will become prevalent in tourism, signalling the advent of a much more differentiated approach to tourism marketing.

Changing values are also generating demand for more environmentally conscious and nature-oriented holidays. Suppliers will therefore have to pay more attention to the way people think, feel and behave than they have done hitherto. In recent years the niche market has become an important factor in the tourism industry reflecting the need to diversify and customize the industry and ensure the sustainability of the product. The main niche markets (sports travel, spas and health care, adventure and nature tourism, cultural tourism, theme parks, cruise ships, religious travel and others) hold great potential and are developing rapidly.

The growth of the cruise tourism sector is an interesting case in point. Between 1980 and 1999, the cruise industry grew at an average annual rate of 7.9 percent. 13 The Caribbean is the most important geographic market for the cruise industry, accounting for over half of all cruises taken in 1996. Since 1984, cruise visitor arrivals have increased every year except 1987 and 1989. In addition, between 1996 and 2000, the growth rate for cruise arrivals is expected to far exceed that of stay-over arrivals. The rapid growth and development of the cruise tourism industry opens key opportunities but also poses a number of threats to their Caribbean destinations. The environmental and economic impacts of cruise tourism are increasingly the subject of discussion. Moreover, given the pace and magnitude of its development, the cruise industry is directly competing with land-based tourism and, as a result, poses a growing threat to hotels and other land-based resorts and businesses in the Caribbean.

Technology in Tourism

On the demand side, consumer preferences for flexible travel and leisure services provide a strong impetus for new tourism. On the supply side, technology plays an important complementary role in engineering new tourism. The applications of technology to the travel and tourism industry allow producers to supply new and flexible services that are cost-competitive with conventional mass, standardized and rigidly packaged options. Technology gives suppliers the flexibility to react to market demands and the capacity to integrate diagonally with other suppliers to provide new combinations of services and improve cost effectiveness.

In the travel and tourism industry a whole range of interrelated computer and communication technologies is being introduced. The system of information technologies (SIT) comprises computerized reservation systems, teleconferencing, video text, videos, video brochures, computers, management information systems, airline electronic information systems, electronic funds transfer systems, digital telephone networks, smart cards, satellite printers, and mobile communications. Each technology component identified in the SIT – for example, computers – can be and usually is fully integrated with the other components. For example, computer-to-computer communications allow hotels to integrate their front offices, back offices and food and beverage operations. This internal management system for hotels can in turn be fully integrated with a digital telephone network, and they then together provide the basis for linkage with hotel reservation systems which can be accessed by travel agents through their computerized reservations terminals (CRTs). Computerized reservations systems have emerged as the dominant technology among others being diffused throughout the travel and tourism industry. In the United States, travel agents are using satellite printers at corporate offices to issue tickets directly at the point of demand. Interactive automated ticket machines (ATMs) have also been introduced. These consist of a computer with an attached printer that enables passengers to research schedules and fares, make reservations, purchase tickets and obtain boarding passes without the intervention of a human agent.

The Internet is a global network connecting millions of computers. As of 1999, the number of Internet users was above 200 million worldwide, and that number is growing rapidly, involving more than 100 countries. It is estimated that there were 63 million World Wide Web users in Europe in 1999. The United Kingdom, with almost 13 million Internet users, currently registers the highest number of users among the European countries. Use of the Internet for travel booking and planning is increasing rapidly. The rapid diffusion of information technologies throughout the travel and tourism industry is expected to improve the efficiency of production and the quality of services provided to consumers, and to generate increasing demand for new services.

The Driving Forces of Globalization Impacting upon Travel, Hospitality and Tourism

Liberalization of Air Transport

The air transport industry, which is located mainly in the industrialized regions and in the newly industrialized countries, is a key determinant in the development of tourism. It is expanding twice as fast as the general output of the world economy, with further growth potential expected over the next two decades. In the developing countries, air transport accounts for nearly 80 percent of international tourist arrivals. In 1998, the industry provided 28 million jobs worldwide, and by 2010 the number of people travelling by air could exceed 2.3 billion each year, with over 31 million jobs provided.

Today, liberalization of air transport largely means market access for private carriers and cabotage rights. The liberalization of air transport, traditionally pursued at the bilateral level, is now being carried to the level of multilateral trade agreements. The recent trend towards the liberalization of air transport notably through the proliferation of open skies agreements, has thus raised the issue of air transport liberalization as a discipline to be debated in the framework of the General Agreement on Trade in Services (GATS).

Multi-bilateral negotiations are already under way on an open skies agreement between the European Union and the United States. If they succeed, 70 percent of the world's international air traffic will be covered by the agreement. It is expected in that case that the agreement will serve as a model for other international air services agreements.

The formation of international alliances is an important development in the field of aviation. Airline alliances have become widespread and are still evolving, with partnership relationships becoming more intertwined and complex. The major airlines in the Americas and Europe are the most active in securing alliance agreements.

The main motivation behind such alliances is the need to minimize costs while maintaining the quality of global services and extending connections throughout the world. Alliances can take various forms including: cooperative arrangements; wide-ranging strategic alliances, most notably the so-called "megaalliances"; groupings and concentrations at national level, as in the case of the United States; purchase or franchising of small regional companies by major operators to carry their customers to hub airports; and regional civil aviation markets.

Other trends which characterize the changes under way in the context of airline liberalization include: partial or full privatization and restructuring of government-owned airlines; partial foreign ownership of airlines; equity investment in foreign carriers; updating of airline alliances by cancelling outdated or non-performing agreements; airline consolidations at the national level; joint ventures, either between airline companies or between airline companies and equipment manufacturers or independent maintenance companies; and outsourcing with no provision of maintenance service.

Some Results of Airline Liberalization

Recent privatization initiatives have ended the protection of national airlines by governments in a number of developing countries. However, the possibility of the market becoming dominated by a single private company is perceived as a serious risk. In some cases, developing countries that have liberalized their air transport sectors as part of a policy to promote tourism have found themselves dominated by one or two foreign airlines.

Some bankruptcies and closures have taken place in countries where distressed national airlines were not or could not be rescued by governments. In this context, a review of the GATS annex on air transport services is intended to draw international attention to the need to design a system that enables developing countries to compete effectively in the world market for air transport.

With regard to the liberalization of air transport as a whole, the trend is increasingly for each State to choose its own pace of change, using bilateral, regional or multilateral mechanisms. 9 In developed countries there has been a clear tightening of competition policies to prohibit governments from providing subsidies. 10 It is well known that many bilateral agreements have resulted in inefficiency as they were based on market access restrictions, price control and protection of money-losing carriers.

Full liberalization of air services as implemented in 1997 in Europe boosted the development of "low-cost" services and their integration in the European aviation scene. Although these services still account for a rather small share of the passenger market, their marketing impact is increasingly being felt throughout the industry. It is estimated that around 25 percent of passengers on United States domestic services use "low-cost" airlines, as compared to approximately 5 percent in Europe.

Another result of liberalization is that new route opportunities have opened up, stimulating new demands without tampering with major carriers' shares and therefore creating new opportunities for fare reductions. Some major European flag carriers have already created their own "low-cost" airline subsidiaries (examples are British Airways/Go and KLM/Buzz).

The low-cost market as it stands has considerable growth potential. Europe's low-cost airlines are finding plenty of untapped markets. Both Ryanair and easyJet have placed orders for significant numbers of additional aircraft to almost double their capacity over the next four years to meet this new demand. The challenge for low-cost carriers is to strike the right balance between maintaining low costs, low prices and high aircraft utilization and establishing a presence at a certain minimum number of airports. A further development of the concept of the low-cost airline sector has been the advent of "seat-only" sales on charter airline flights, rather than as part of a package holiday. This has resulted, for example, in the formation of the European Leisure Group (ELG), an alliance of European charter and scheduled airlines.

Liberalization of Trade in Services Negotiations on Tourism Services and Existing Commitments Under the GATS

The General Agreement on Trade in Services (GATS) became part of the "New World Trade Order" under the aegis of the World Trade Organization as established by the Uruguay Round in 1994. The functioning of GATS is based on the interplay of fundamental standards in commercial law, procedural regulations for their implementation and specific commitments in which member States document sector-specific limitations or concessions. GATS has universal coverage and includes a comprehensive definition of trade in services comprising four "modes of supply".

The tourism sector had already undergone various forms of liberalization before the Uruguay Round. It is also considered to be one of the service sectors most liberalized through sector-specific commitments made by signatory States. The number of commitments by the World Trade Organization members made so far in tourism under the GATS is rated as the highest of all sectors. Of 127 GATS signatory States, only eight have not made commitments in tourism and travel related services. In the hotels and restaurants subsector, which offers the greatest potential for far-reaching liberalization within tourism, it is mostly low and lowermiddle- income economies (LIEs and LMIEs according to the World Bank classification) in Africa and Latin America that have liberalized market access for foreign investors in the *"commercial presence"* mode: 64 percent of all signatory States belonging to the group of LIEs and 75 percent of LMIEs, but only about half (48 percent) of the group of high-income economies (HIEs) have "no restrictions" to that mode.

On the other hand, it is not surprising that *"presence of natural persons"* is the least liberalized mode of supply: in 117 of the 119 countries signing commitments in travel and tourism-related services, there are restrictions on the movement of hotel staff. Sixty-eight countries refer to their non-sector specific commitments which mostly offer only temporary stay for business visitors, intra-corporate transferees and professionals. This mode is the key starting point for future moves to shift liberalization away from declaring countries' restrictive measures towards removing those measures. It is expected that the next round of GATS talks will have important repercussions on destinations in terms of tourism marketing, investment and ownership, training and other aspects affecting the structure of the industry.

The case for a more specific treatment of tourism services under the GATS has been the subject of debate since the conclusion of the Uruguay Round. Significantly, UNCTAD has come up with conclusions and recommendations with regard to the future round of negotiations on trade in tourism under the GATS, including a recommendation and a proposal for an annex on tourism services called for by the World Trade Organization. So far, tourism is not among the specific sectors referred to by the six annexes of the GATS and other related instruments. Only an ancillary service to tourism (airline computer reservation services), is included in an annex on air transport services.

Economic Integration

The world economy is currently witnessing two distinct trends– globalization and regionalization – and within this context States as well as companies are pursuing a variety of different strategies in order to become more competitive. Shifting patterns of production and consumption across the world are also reflected in the rise of new international tourism destinations, particularly in the East Asia and Pacific region. This has given rise to increasing regional, intra-regional and interregional competition and to new challenges in terms of investment needs and human resources development, especially with regard to training and labour mobility.

The impact of trade blocs on the hotel, tourism and catering sector can be gauged by the strategies adopted to create an environment conducive to tourism development. The European Union has launched a wide range of initiatives and activities through a variety of programmes in such broad areas as sustainable development, dissemination of information, training and enterprise promotion. The main thrust of social policy in the European Union is the improvement of labour market conditions with a special focus on those excluded from the labour market and the unemployed. European Union labour laws and social policy are having a positive impact on the tourism sector. Of importance here is the Maastricht Social Protocol which has benefited seasonal and part-time workers and small businesses. Other policies that have proved beneficial to the development of tourism include the free movement of workers across Europe, harmonization of qualifications and tax incentives for education and training.

The North American Free Trade Agreement (NAFTA) benefits the travel and tourism industry in many ways. It promotes demand for direct air and charter/tour bus travel in the region, guarantees that tourism companies will receive national treatment in all three countries and maintains high quality of tourism services by encouraging the expansion of telecommunications links between the United States and Mexico.

Mercosur is, in economic terms, the world's fourth largest trade bloc, covering a population of 205 million people. Economic integration, through the practice of free trade with no tariff or pretariff restrictions between the member States of the bloc, has led to increasing cross-border flows of labour, goods and investment. Mercosur's concern is to tackle labour relations, employment and social security issues and the short-term negative effects of integration on labour in the member States.

Tourism development is a priority on the agenda of the Association of South- East Asian Nations (ASEAN). Its development strategy incorporates: promotion of sustainable tourism development; preservation of cultural and environmental resources; provision of transportation and other infrastructure; simplification of immigration procedures; and human resources development. A plan of action on ASEAN cooperation in tourism shows the emphasis that is being placed on investment in human resources development, with a special focus on tourism education and training with a view to upgrading the skills needed to meet the demand for improved service quality and professionalism in the tourism and travel industry and thereby sustain ASEAN's overall competitive advantage. Cooperation in tourism education and training is being intensified through the sharing of resources, skills and training facilities provided by tourism training institutions through technical assistance and experts.

Information and Communication Technologies in the HCT Sector

Computerized reservation systems (CRSs) have been developed by large air carriers since the 1970s to process flight reservations, but have evolved and expanded over time to provide other air transport-related services. Each airline has its own CRS and they are interconnected through global distribution systems (GDSs). A huge number of Internet on-line reservation systems act as a kind of virtual agent, most of them having direct links to one or several CRS/GDS. The CRS and GDS systems have become the main distribution and marketing tool in the international tourism trade and have greatly enhanced the efficiency of travel agents' business operations. They cater to the needs of different market segments, including management of air and land transport services, the hospitality sector and entertainment services, as well as other ancillary services which make commercial transactions and risk coverage feasible. As a result, they have become increasingly important and are extensively used by all suppliers of tourism services.

There is some concern that developing countries' suppliers may well be left out because GDSs can present major barriers to entry owing to their unfavourable access conditions (their operational costs, problems of access for small service suppliers, the fact that they are owned by large air carriers). A number of

African and south Asian countries are poorly represented in these systems because of structural handicaps such as the low level of tourism development in general and their underdeveloped hospitality sector.

The poor representation of small service suppliers in GDSs adversely affects the dissemination of information on their tourism products, thereby holding back their sale and marketing of tourism services. This leaves such suppliers, especially SMEs, at a competitive disadvantage compared with those who are represented in the major GDSs. GDSs in many developing countries, particularly in Africa, are established in the form of joint ventures with local partners – for example, the national carrier – but operate within a de facto monopoly.

This leads to excessive user fees and hinders their potential for developing tourism. Travel agents in developing countries are at a disadvantage with regard to the use of modern technology compared with their counterparts in developed countries because of poor information network infrastructure and the shortage of professionals to manage, operate and maintain the system. Human resources assume importance in the operation of GDSs and other electronic media, and this calls for staff training in mastering the systems and their application to marketing, through specific training programmes provided by both the public and private sectors.

Emerging Use of the Internet for Marketing and Sales

Deregulation, globalization and radical shifts in leisure and tourism behaviour on the demand side have driven the tourism industry towards information-oriented activities, as seen in the introduction of IT systems in a wide range of spheres in the tourism and leisure sector.

The increasing use of the Internet for destination marketing, direct sales and bookings has given rise to electronic tourism markets and at present tourism is among the most important application domains in the World Wide Web. The development of websites has made possible the direct delivery of comprehensive travel information about tourism suppliers to potential travellers.

Text-based websites with photos and graphics linked to websites of tourism suppliers at the destination is another innovative approach to marketing.

Developing an effective travel website has now assumed importance for obvious reasons. International tourists are increasingly using the travel websites on the Internet that were launched by most international companies in the late 1990s. However, the real volume of Internet bookings can only be estimated and estimates from market research companies are contradictory. According to one estimate, between 33 and 50 percent of Internet transactions are tourism based. Available evidence show that as yet only a tiny percentage of business travellers are booking on-line. On-line sales in Europe, for example, represented only 0. 1 percent of the European travel market, and in 1999 only 1 percent of the world's airline tickets, hotel and other bookings were purchased over the Internet, although the proportion of airline and other ticket sales through the Internet is expected to grow sharply over the next three to four years.

The Internet helps to make travel products globally accessible at much lower cost – without transaction costs and the costs of intermediaries – and has comparatively low entrance barriers with regard to financial resources and human know-how. For many suppliers, tourism marketing efforts are increasingly focusing on Internet users.

A new business environment and new ways of doing business have sprung up as a result of the accessibility and relatively low cost of the Internet which is bringing businesses and consumers, buyers and suppliers on-line. Internet and Internet protocol technology is the driving force behind the growth of e-business. The Internet will have repercussions on business in the areas of e-commerce, e-working and e-procurement. A recent global survey of more than 500 business leaders lends support to the idea that e-business will be a key factor in competitive advantage in the future.

In the sphere of air travel, attempts are frequently made to bypass traditional travel agencies by direct booking via the Internet or corporate implant offices. Customer demands are becoming more technology driven, such as the demand for professional travel and billing management in place of mere ticket issuing. Advances in technology in the hotels and tourism industry, as exemplified by readily available information to guests and employees, faster service delivery, shorter cycle times and more dynamic markets, also require prompt action from service suppliers if marketing opportunities are not to be lost. Strategies of growth and concentration through mergers and acquisitions are becoming increasingly important from the mediators' perspective as a response to cost and performance pressures in international business travel. In addition, traditional kick-back contracts are increasingly being replaced with new performance-oriented arrangements.

All aspects of business are being reshaped by the Internet and its related technologies, intranets and extranets. Hospitality enterprises will need to focus on providing customers with real-time access to rates and product information. The Internet also provides hotels and restaurants with opportunities to redesign the way in which they interface with employees and suppliers.

The high growth in global commerce accompanied by the emergence of electronic commerce driven mainly by the Internet has raised concerns about the need to regulate cyberspace by setting standards to regulate the use of the Internet for all aspects of travel and other fast-growing categories of electronic commerce. The primacy of the rules of the network economy will significantly lower transaction and communication costs, thus allowing more flexible pricing. The regulation of the Internet through the enactment and implementation of cyber-laws and privacy standards will most probably be perceived as an encouraging initiative which will guarantee safety and security in Internet business transactions, especially in shopping and travel accommodation bookings, where the Internet is most frequently used.

As a way of managing the increasing volume of guest information, the introduction of data warehousing and data mining technologies is becoming increasingly important. Hoteliers and restaurateurs have already expressed marked interest in these technologies as means of exploiting the advantages which can be derived from, for example, increased guest loyalty and market share. By using data warehousing and data mining as well as the Internet, the hotel industry can provide higher levels of personalized services and value.

The Internet is turning out to be the most sought after amenity in hotel rooms, providing communications access, information, entertainment and education. It enables more self-service oriented transactions to take place, especially in the area of reservations booking. Information technology impacts on all aspects of the hotel organization value chain and transcends all departmental and geographical boundaries. Decisions on technology-related issues need to be made at top management levels of companies, and this means that qualified information technology personnel are needed at those levels.

Another key issue is the source of investment capital required to fund information technology initiatives. Lack of capital seriously hinders the implementation of information technology and competition for fund sourcing. The Internet has brought about some very significant technological changes that enhance its capabilities and viability and its potential to drive electronic commerce. Besides introducing new and innovative business models in both the business-to-business and business-to-consumer markets, the Internet has shortened the value chain and put pressure on all players, especially intermediaries, by giving rise to the so-called "disintermediation" process, that is, the elimination of intermediary organizations such as travel agencies and global distribution systems (GDSs). These intermediary organizations are gradually being replaced by new emerging intermediaries.

On-line service and ticketless travel have significantly reduced the need for travel intermediaries, as a result of which travel agents in the United States, for example, have seen a reduction in commissions paid to them by airlines. The use of information technology in the tourism industry is determined by such factors as the scale and complexity of tourism demand and the degree of expansion and sophistication of new tourism products. Tourism plays an important role in a significant number of developing countries, many of which enjoy a competitive advantage. Current changes in the hotel and tourism industry in the context of globalization, as described in this report, show that there are more opportunities in the field of e-commerce than in any other existing technology which developing countries can exploit to their advantage in order to improve the marketing of their tourism products. However, in the developing countries, tourism development is constrained by a number of factors which have been summarized by UNCTAD.

Computer software represents one of the largest segments of services delivered through the cross-border mode of supply, with a growing number of developing countries using the Internet both to market and to deliver these services. The Indian software industry is a case in point.

Electronic commerce facilitates access to new markets, as well as being cost saving and time saving. However, its effectiveness depends to a large extent on the establishment of a sound telecommunications infrastructure; in most low-income countries, that infrastructure is inadequate. A wide range of factors prevent the great majority of developing countries from accessing foreign markets through the Internet. Those factors include monopoly pricing for long-distance telephony, uncertainty about the regulatory environment, lack of human resources, lack of awareness among developing country companies of the relevance of the digital economy, and the high cost of setting up, upgrading and redesigning a significant e-commerce site. The status of the developing countries' readiness for e-commerce is an important issue.

Providers of tourism services must also have the capacity to invest in or have access to the physical infrastructure for logistics services and information technologies. The major obstacle to increased use of e-commerce in developing countries is the lack of pervasive low-cost telecommunications, broadcasting, Internet services and associated infrastructures, especially in rural areas. At the same time there is a need to involve more hotel and tourism enterprises from developing countries in the actual use of information technologies and information networks. If African businesses fare better than consumers in terms of accessing e-commerce, they nevertheless face the same infrastructure problems, although progress has been made in the development of e-commerce activities.

The shortage of IT specialists on the market, especially in the developing countries, is a serious impediment, given the rapid growth in Internet use. The demand for IT skills is increasing and the need for retraining of existing employees in both the public and private sectors in hotels, tourism and catering is clearly felt. One solution would be for developing countries to take advantage of forthcoming GATS negotiations to ensure access for their suppliers to the most important generating markets, and they could make use of certain mechanisms provided for in the GATS which might enhance the contribution of trade in services to development. They could also seek commitments with respect to the training of personnel and access to the distribution channels which are essential to tourism exports, as provided for in Articles IV and XIX of the Agreement.

Consolidation Strategies

Since the mid-1990s, multinational hotel companies entering foreign markets have devised a wide range of management strategies or methods in response to competitive challenge such as the rapid development of information technology, sophisticated demands from well-informed and knowledgeable travellers and the rise of electronic business-to-business market-places and to seize the opportunities opened up by the network economy. Within each company, core competencies are being developed and renewed through rapid information technology development, international expansion and market cooperation, relationship management, development of customer-oriented products and services, structural re-engineering (involving, for example, organizational restructuring and continuous training of employees and management), new marketing initiatives and campaigns, and quality control.

According to the IH&RA, multinational hotel companies have invested heavily in developing customer-oriented technology services and enhancing management information and operation systems.

Within the context of international expansion and market cooperation, companies have had recourse to a number of competitive methods which merit attention. The growing number of alliances is changing industry structures and the level of competition has shifted from the individual company level to alliance groups level. The last five years have witnessed nine major mergers and acquisition transactions in the international hotel market-place. For example, Hilton and Hilton International have merged their sales forces, integrated their logos and marketing efforts, and shared their reservation systems in a strategic alliance considered to be the largest since 1996. Hilton has also allied with Patriot American Hospitality for market expansion. Starwood has established a strategic alliance with Discovery Hotel Group in Asia to open Four Points Hotels in China. Choice International has done the same with Flag International in Asia.

There are other goals and objectives which strategic alliances can fulfil in order to assist multinational hotel firms in strengthening their market positions, improving partnership relations and supplying diversified products and quality services to their customers.

These goals and objectives include: acquisition of new information and communication technology (Hyatt and Starwood with Microsoft's Expedia, Hyatt with MSN network, Carlson and Bass with WizCom to link to global distribution systems); distribution of products and cross-marketing between food-service providers and hotels (Ramada with Bennigan's Restaurants, Marriott, Hilton, Bass with Pizza Hut); distribution and cross-promotion of bank credit cards and financial services between banks and hotels (Bass Hotels and Resorts with Visa and American Express, Marriot with Visa and Chase Manhattans processing system, Hilton, Starwood, and Accor with American Express); consolidation of transportation and hotel services (Carlson and Bass Hotels and Resorts each with more than 20 airlines, Marriott with United Airlines, Starwood with British Airways and Alitalia, and Shangri-la with Canadian Airlines); co-promotion of hotels and films and media (Marriott, Choice Hotels and Cendant with new films, Bass with ESPN and Discovery Channel, and Best Western with Sci-Fi Channel and E-Entertainment Channel).

Management contracts are popular competitive methods that are being used by international companies. A good example is that of Nikko Hotels International which through its expansion into Croatia acquired 21 management contracts in 1998. Some well established international companies provide their expertise by leasing out management teams to run local firms. The contracting company benefits from the knowledge and experience of the international company and from its reputation for quality and good service. Quoting figures from Ankomah (1991), Becherel and Cooper point out that in 1979, 72 percent of all hotels in sub-Saharan Africa operated under a management contract; in Asia the figure was 60 percent, in Latin America 47 percent, but only 2 percent in Europe. It can be assumed that these proportions have increased with globalization.

Franchising – a contractual agreement whereby one company allows another to sell and use its products for a fee – presents a number of advantages upon which many multinational hotel companies rely for their growth and expansion. From a local human resources perspective, franchising offers the advantage of recruiting local management and staff with the added benefit of the expertise of the franchiser and any good international practice. This method of market entry is favoured by some of the international hotel corporations.

Their international reputation guarantees licensees a ready-made market. In Europe, for example, franchising accounts for 1.5 million jobs, the majority in France, Germany and the United Kingdom. Many franchise agreements have been signed in the past five years. What is more, companies which have not in the past espoused franchising as an expansion tool have started to use it to the full. This was the case with Hyatt and Marriott in 1995 and 1996.

Many joint ventures or partnerships were set up between 1995 and 1996. Some examples are: Choice International with Friendly Hotels in the United Kingdom; Cendant with Mark's Hotel International's cooperation agreement in India; Accor with NH Hotels in Spain, Starwood with Hotel Pelikan in Germany and Demeure Hotels in Europe; and Sol Melia with European Travel.

The emergence of branding is another new issue in the hotel industry which is linked to merger and acquisition activities. With the evolution of the hotel industry towards a more consumer-oriented service, it is the brand rather than the company which assumes importance. In the United Kingdom hotel industry, for example, branding has become very topical and operators are increasingly recognizing the value of brands in delivering profits. The brand is thus turning out to be a fundamental element in defining the market, so much so that it is the name of the brand under which a hotel trades that carries weight, rather than its ownership and management structure. The emergence of a multiplicity of new brand names worldwide in the last five years – Cendant's Wingate Inn, Accor's Studio 6, Hilton's Garden Inn, and others – bears testimony to its increasing importance.

All these developments indicate the extent to which new products and services – including the other new competitive methods and customer-oriented technologies mentioned earlier – that have been launched by multinational hotel companies are being developed in an attempt to sustain their respective competitive advantage. Vertical integration is another strategy that plays a dominant role in particular segments of the tourism industry. For a long time, tour operators have been establishing backward and forward linkages in the areas of service production. Their backward integration includes hotels and charter airlines. These operators also control all stages of distribution via far-reaching forward integration of retail distributors and travel agencies, marketing and package tours sales. This is also true of airlines which extend their level of integration far into the field of primary tourism and travel-related services via their charter airlines which have interests in tour operators, retailers and travel agencies. By contrast, hotels and hotel chains hardly pursue vertical integration strategies at all.

Tour operators and travel agencies are becoming increasingly involved in the process of horizontal integration, which in the recent past has attracted attention through spectacular takeovers like that of Thomas Cook by the German LTU group in 1993, or through joint ventures. An expansionist strategy of diagonal integration is geared to the provision of the broadest possible array of tourism-related service markets by a company, with a view to cutting costs, making the most of synergies between individual markets and achieving systems gains. This includes, for example, the joint use of computerized reservation systems by carriers and travel agencies under the umbrella of a holding company or cooperation between credit card suppliers and tour operators or travel agencies offering the special insurance services of a holding partner.

In the accommodation industry, an impressive amount of consolidation took place in the 1980s, bringing more and more hotel brands under fewer and larger corporate umbrellas. Consolidation offers certain advantages such as cost reduction in the areas of reservation systems, loyalty programmes and staff training and other fixed costs associated with hotel management. Available figures reinforce the impression that the forces of consolidation are indeed gathering momentum. In the institutional catering sector, franchising and management contracts are also used as management strategies by institutional food-service companies.

Compass, which is among the largest institutional catering companies in the world, employing 125,000 workers in 44 countries, is a case in point. It owns, manages or franchises hotels (Forte, Meridien, Posthouse, Heritage and Travelodge). Its food service brands include Burger King, Sbarro, Upper Crust, Caffe Ritazza, Delimento, Little Chef and Harry Ramsdens. In Canada, the institutional catering sector is dominated by large international groups. Sodexho is the largest institutional catering company, employing 212,000 employees worldwide since it purchased the institutional catering services of Marriott – Marriott Services. Another example is Aramak, an American company which employ 140,000 employees in 11 countries based in North America and Europe.

One pertinent issue frequently referred to by the developing countries is the need to reduce the risk of "leakage" of foreign exchange earnings. The developing countries in particular are usually unable to make the most of the economic and development potential of tourism, firstly, because of the high import content of construction materials and equipment and consumable goods needed to cater to the needs of international tourism and, secondly, because of the repatriation of income and profits earned by expatriates. The latter is in fact a major obstacle to tourism development.

Nevertheless, a number of advantages can be derived from international companies in terms of capital investment and know-how and technology, management and marketing expertise, training and consultancy. For example, under the "Build Operate Transfer" model, there may be conditions attached such as the requirement to train local staff or build facilities for the community. This enables countries lacking the skills base and expertise needed at all professional levels to run, develop and operate tourist establishments for an international clientele to benefit from the transfer of expertise and technology. In a globalized economy, skills become an important determinant in competitiveness. The changing composition of the workforce and work patterns resulting from globalization processes in the industry have brought about new challenges in human resources development. Training policies in the hotel, tourism and catering sector will need to be reviewed in a new climate of empowerment and retention of staff. This is particularly the case in many parts of the world where there is an acute shortage of qualified staff to fill positions created by an expanding industry. An internationally focused human resources policy calls for a change in personnel policies and strategies which implies, among other things, management commitment to transnational strategies, the development of IT skills and procedures to support transnational operations in a number of ways such as knowledge and information transfer, and an awareness of the different national policies on health and safety, occupational standards, dismissal, discrimination and workers' rights.

Impact of Technology on SMEs

Globalization has brought about a range of opportunities and challenges which have put additional pressures on SMEs. In addition to having to cope with the effects of globalization, they need to adapt to new business conditions in terms of product positioning and product development facilitated by information technology, with all its potential benefits in terms of market access for SMEs. The potential of SMEs for achieving economies of scale is very limited and the use of computer reservation systems (CRSs) has not spread significantly, quite apart from the fact that SMEs are already disadvantaged because of their high average unit production costs. SMEs are forced by market conditions to install new systems and train their staff to use tourism-related technology but find it difficult to invest in training or staff development, mainly because of limited investment resources and the fact that many SMEs in the hotel, tourism and catering sector are managed by a generation of staff have had no formal training in the sector.

In a globalized market, SMEs need to pursue new survival strategies. The tourism sector at the destination has to cope with the increasing problem of seasonality encountered by many coastal resorts. Competitive advantage then depends on organizational competencies and capabilities. Local SMEs have to face a number of conditions imposed by large overseas companies. Large tour operators strongly influence the way in which hotels operate at their featured destinations and the prices that they charge, particularly in mass market beach resorts and in short season resorts (e.g. ski resorts); they may also impose conditions on local suppliers, such as compliance with environmental protection standards.

In developing countries, SMEs play an important role in employment creation but are hampered by low productivity levels, poor product quality and lack of access to credit and training. The impact of capital outflows from developing countries resulting from e-commerce is another issue which needs attention. The need to develop competition policy-related disciplines in this area is also clearly felt, in view of the need to establish safeguards to prevent abuse by dominant suppliers. Such issues arising from e-commerce might be addressed in future GATS negotiations.

The global hotel market encompasses a wide range of types of accommodation – full-service hotels, bed and breakfast inns, suites, self-catering short-term apartments and time-share properties. Distribution and intermediation are increasingly recognized as factors critical to the competitiveness and success of the tourism industry in general and of small and medium-sized tourism enterprises in particular.

The latter need to develop effective distribution channels either to meet the needs of their independent clientele or to provide direct booking mechanisms to reduce their dependency on tour operators. Hospitality organizations and hotel chains already rely on customer bookings through the Internet. The challenge for tourism sector SMEs is to be able to compete for their market shares and take advantage of emerging opportunities and associated benefits to enhance their profitability and viability in the global market-place.

Cost and benefit analysis for developing Internet presence for small and medium-sized tourism enterprises Costs;

- Costs of purchasing hardware, software and communication package
- Training cost of users
- Design and construction of Internet presence
- Cost of hosting the site on a reliable server
- Ongoing maintenance and regular updating
- Marketing the Internet service and registration of domains
- Development of procedures for dealing with Internet presence
- Commissions for purchases on-line by intermediaries
- Advertising fees for representation in search engines and other sites
- Interconnectivity with travel intermediaries such as TravelWeb, ITN, Expedia.

Benefits

- Direct bookings, often intermediaries and commission free
- Global distribution of multimedia information and promotional material
- Low cost of providing and distributing timely updates of information

- Global presence on the Internet, 24 hours a day, 365 days a year
- Durability of promotion (in comparison to limited life of printed advertising in press)
- Reduction of promotional cost and reduction of brochure waste
- Great degree of attention by visitors to website
- Reduction of time required for transactions and ability to offer last minute promotions
- Low marginal cost of providing information to additional users
- Support of marketing intelligence and product design functions
- Development of targeted mailing lists through people who actively request information
- Great interactivity with prospective customers
- Niche marketing to prospective consumers who request to receive information
- Interactivity with local partners and provision of added value products at destinations
- Ability to generate a community feel for current users and prospective customers.

SMEs in the tourism sector are constrained by the growing concentration and globalization of tourism supply. In addition, lack of professionalism and inadequate management and marketing skills, the absence of economies of scale and limited access to the necessary capital, human resources, marketing expertise and technology, over-reliance on a limited number of distribution partners and inadequate formal education or business training are among other deficiencies which put them at a competitive disadvantage. Overall, the inability to market their products adequately seriously affects their profitability and ability to survive in the globalized economy.

SMEs are highly reliant on existing distribution channels, namely, intermediaries such as tour operators, travel agencies, travel information centres and tourist guides. It can be argued that the gradual reduction of SMEs' reliance on intermediaries will enable them to become more profitable, flexible and adaptable and to produce customized tourism products in order to satisfy niche markets. This will also require a rethink of all strategic and operational practices with regard to SME development, as well as development of entrepreneurs' managerial skills and professionalism, training in marketing and management and on the use of information technology.

SMEs can benefit in a number of ways by applying information technology to develop their product, thereby enhancing their market position and increasing their profit margins. Information technology offers new management and business opportunities and can be applied strategically to gain competitive advantage, improve productivity and performance, facilitate new ways of managing and organizing, and develop new businesses.

Although information technology entails risks and costs, its underutilization could increase the vulnerability of SMEs and aggravate any competitive disadvantage as greater use is made of IT systems, including CRSs, GDSs and the Internet, to locate and purchase tourism and accommodation products. 56 With regard to electronic data interchange (EDI), for example, empirical evidence suggests that EDI is perceived by SMEs as too complex and cumbersome and that the initial investment is too high.

Although SMEs play a major role in the international tourism and hotel industry, their vulnerability becomes quite obvious in the highly demanding business environment characterized by competition generated by globalization and the transformation of tourism demand. Globalization of the industry means that SMEs in the tourism sector compete in a multinational environment where only organizations capable of providing exceptional value or cost advantage will survive.

The opportunity of achieving economies of scale in distribution channels, reservations, marketing, advertising, administration, personnel management, technology adaptation, new product development, training and bulk purchasing of raw material and equipment, has been instrumental in the creation of major hotel chains, international consortia, management contracts and multinational franchising companies, and has placed the independent operator at a disadvantage. The overall trend in the hotel industry appears to be towards a gradual but steady switch from independently owned and operated hotels to hotel chains. SMEs seem to be the weakest and most vulnerable members of the industry and will need to seek competitive advantages if they are to compete and maintain their market share in an increasingly globalized economy.

Employment and Working Conditions

Composition of the Labour Force

Worldwide, employment within the tourism economy is estimated at 192.2 million jobs (one in every 12.4 jobs in the formal sector). By 2010, this should grow to 251.6 million jobs (one in every 11 formal sector jobs). This includes employment created by fixed capital formation activities and by providers to the tourism industry. Direct employment for tourist consumption amounts to about 3 percent of total employment worldwide. In some countries, however, the proportion is three times higher (Spain – 8.3 percent; Mauritius – 10 percent; Barbados – 10.5 percent). The industry is heavily dominated by SMEs: in Europe, for example, there are 2.7 million SMEs operating in the sector, representing almost all HCT enterprises. Some 94 percent of this segment are micro-enterprises employing fewer than ten people. SMEs employ over half the labour force working in the industry.

Although tourism is a growth industry and a major creator of value added, the industry is vulnerable to a variety of economic, ecological, geopolitical and meteorological factors, and over-reliance on it can be dangerous for a country. Economic recession and the impact of natural disasters or terrorist attacks can devastate the sector in a country for several years. One example is the recent Asian financial crisis which resulted in a substantial tourism downturn throughout 1997 and 1998 in affected countries, which have only recently started to recover.

Another is the war in the Balkans, which has seriously reduced tourism income in that area. Events of this kind represent the extremes of a recurrent uncertainty in an industry which is characterized by the seasonal nature of many of its activities and by important fluctuations even during normal periods. These factors shape the structure of the tourism labour force, making it difficult to maintain high permanent staffing levels. There is a generic tendency to operate on the basis of a core staff and to employ the labour needed for day-to-day operations under atypical contractual arrangements.

As the ultimate "just in time" deliverer of goods and services, the restaurant sector has to face exceptional peaks of work as, to a lesser degree, does the hotel sector – either during holiday periods or, for example, to deal with congresses. The industry responds by maintaining a large pool of temporary labour on which it can draw in response to demand. These workers are likely to be young and/or female. The necessary availability is often found among students wishing to combine university or vocational studies with flexible working hours in hotels and restaurants. The industry employs mostly young people, and indeed for many of them provides the point of entry into the world of work. Women may also find flexible arrangements convenient as a means of balancing family obligations and work. The available statistics show that the industry also has a high proportion of female employees.

The prevailing patterns of the HCT workforce are illustrated by the following statistics:

- a study by the National Restaurant Association in the United States, 3 based on 1996 data, found that 52 percent of restaurant employees in the United States were women, 25 percent of employees were aged between 16 and 19 years, 19 percent were between 20 and 24 years and a further 25 percent were aged between 25 and 34 years;
- in Austria in 1995, women accounted for between 60 and 70 percent of total HCT employment, depending on the subsector, the proportion of women being particularly high in food services and accommodation. In the same country, 14.5 percent of workers in the industry were under 20 years old;

- in the Netherlands, the average age of workers in the industry is 23 years; in Denmark, 50 percent of all employees are under 30 years old; in Spain, over 50 percent of all employees are under 34 years old, and the 16-24 years age group represents 20.4 percent of total employment in the sector;
- some 58 percent of workers in the hospitality sector in Australia are women; in Denmark, the industry is 62 percent female; in Italy there is a 50 percent split between men and women; in the Netherlands 52 percent of employees are women; and, although in Spain the figure is 42.5 percent, the number of women employed in the sector is increasing.

In an industry which employs a large proportion of young, mobile people, turnover is bound to be high, and recruitment is a habitual problem in the sector for this and other reasons. However, one hotel in the United Kingdom has introduced a customer host scheme, under which older recruits – with a minimum age of 55, but generally over 60 – are recruited to help out as concierges during peak periods. Such employees often have considerable experience in the industry and may have a lower absentee rate. Another example is found in the Canadian accommodation sector, where the workforce is ageing owing to lower turnover in workplaces with better working conditions and wages. One-quarter of the workforce is over 44 years old, and trade unions are starting to negotiate reduced workloads for older employees whose work involves a high degree of physical exertion.

Impact of New Technology on Skills Requirements

Information and communications technology (ICT) systems which integrate the power of the Internet, customer relationship management and supply chain management in a seamless, one-source destination site, allow a variety of operations – product selection, ordering, fulfilment, tracking, payment and reporting – to be performed with one easy-to-use tool. By cutting out one or more layers of the purchasing structure, these systems yield cost savings by putting the buyer in some instances into direct contact with the producer. They also have employment implications, as intermediaries find that their share of the market is shrinking, with inevitable reductions in labour requirements upstream of the HCT sector.

Technology which facilitates on-line hotel, restaurant and theatre reservations or travel arrangements will have an impact in terms of staff reductions on the front-desk hotel staff who used to perform those functions. This technology also calls for a different range of skills from employees. Although systems designers, aware of the rapid turnover among front-desk staff, are working on products that are easier to operate and thus reduce training time for new recruits, the technology is changing so fast that knowledge becomes obsolete ever more quickly. Training will therefore become a continuous need and the remaining jobs will require greater skills.

Many hotels are examining the possibility of installing personal computers in their guest rooms, and some have indeed already done so. This allows customers to use hotel rooms as their offices. Increasing numbers of business guests are also travelling with their own portable computers. Hyatt International Hotels are an example of how new job profiles may be created as a result of this technology.

The group has introduced "technology concierges" in their deluxe properties worldwide. These specialist employees, known within the group as "compcierges", are trained to help guests to set up their mobile communications equipment, to explain how to use the in-room technology, hook up laptop computers, provide support in accessing e-mail or the Internet, and so on.

They may also help to locate local retailers that service computers and stock software. While technological expertise is essential, the emphasis is on service; all the team members come from a hospitality background and have in addition received the training needed to become electronic troubleshooters. ICT equipment installed in hotels also requires maintenance and planning departments, making this a new field with job creation potential, although such work may largely be subcontracted to outside operators. Swissôtel has established an ICT department employing ten people, which is now an independent, profitable element of the company. The Carlson Hospitality Group also has a knowledge technologies division, which was created to ensure the smooth operation of the reservation and customer information systems installed in the group's 600 hotels throughout the world.

The new technology is also being used by a number of companies as a means of raising skills levels. Domino's Pizza has developed interactive, learner-centred programmes to guide young employees through the steps involved in making a pizza. Computer-based coaches will soon be available to guide employees through all stages of customer relations. Companies will invest in these new techniques to fulfil their training needs. Hotel managements are studying technologies which will reduce the attention which guests require from hotel staff.

These include: electronic key cards which will open doors and act as credit cards for all on-site purchases; management systems which record the time guests are likely to check out, so that room service may be programmed more efficiently; and cleaning staff equipped with hand-held computers, linked to the hotel's property management system (PMS), so that information can be centralized and constantly updated in real time. The Canadian Regional Office of the Hotel Employees and Restaurant Employees International Union (HEREIU) has expressed concern that such systems will allow hotel companies to computerize almost all everyday front-office operations.

Where customers can make their own reservations via the Internet, they could replace switchboard operators altogether. HEREIU further maintains that new in-room technologies such as video check-out systems will replace front-line workers, while electronic keys will be able to tell the PMS exactly how long each employee has spent cleaning a room, and may thus tend to promote an aggressive productivity policy.

The International Union of Food, Agricultural, Hotel, Restaurant, Catering, Tobacco and Allied Workers' Associations (IUF) notes that placing the emphasis on time-saving and labour-saving technologies also means that the pace of work is faster, and argues that in reality, "labour-saving" and "time-saving" are inclined to mean reductions in the numbers of workers. In the

IUF's view, the ultimate consequence of time-and-attendance computer software, which provides information on guest arrivals and departures so that workers can be dispatched to their duties immediately, is the dehumanization of work.

New Technologies in Restaurants

New technologies will also result in structural changes in restaurant kitchens. Use of the "sous-vide" technique, where food that has been totally or partially preprepared or pre-cooked is supplied directly to the restaurant, means that a large number of cooking operations can now be outsourced to independent suppliers or to centralized, chain-based kitchens.

New methods of food preservation, such as freezing, drying, irradiation, and vacuum and modified-atmosphere packing, enhance the shelf life of products and further reduce last minute operations. On the other hand, new types of equipment have given the baking process in restaurant kitchens a new lease of life. Suppliers of pre-prepared dough cooperate with the manufacturers of specialized ovens so that restaurant staff are required to do nothing more than place the dough in the ovens, activate the appropriate computer programme and remove the bread when it is ready.

But the tendency of these innovations is to transform restaurant kitchens into assembly lines, with fewer staff members, since both the simple repetitive tasks, such as vegetable preparation, and the more complex, last minute operations, will be outsourced.

Both the HEREIU and the IUF argue that "regenerated pre-processed foods" require fewer skills of kitchen staff and result in the loss of many kinds of food preparation and cooking jobs in the industry.

The IUF also points to a devaluation in wages as a result of the deskilling of the remaining jobs. These arguments are difficult to refute, since most of these technologies provide savings in terms of staffing levels. On the other hand, the technologies could open up crucial empowerment possibilities, freeing staff to deal more attentively with customers, thus enhancing the profile of the establishment.

New Technologies and Travel Agencies

Access to on-line booking via the Internet is causing traditional travel agents considerable problems. It will soon be possible to reserve travel tickets using new mobile phone technology, without the need for a computer. A recent survey carried out by the International Air Transport Association (IATA) revealed that some 37 percent of travellers worldwide had used electronic tickets, while in the United States, 50 percent of travellers expected to use such tickets by the end of 2000.

Some travel agents are responding to this situation by adopting a more entrepreneurial attitude, charging customers a fee instead of the traditional commission earned on a ticket price. However, while agents may retain business contracts, they are likely to lose individual customer business for simple trips, and this drop in trade will have an impact on employment levels in the branch. Other agencies see the future in strengthening their role as consultants capable of planning complicated trips involving numerous and varied travel means and stopoffs. However, while the human element will not disappear, it will probably diminish with the spread of 24-hour "warehouse" travel agents (much as 24-hour banking has developed) which allow customers to call and make their bookings at any time.

Salaries and Wages

According to a 1996 survey by the European Foundation for the Improvement of Living and Working Conditions covering 15 European Union countries, working conditions within the industry included a number of potentially problematic areas, such as irregular working hours, frequent work on Sundays, wages without a fixed basic element in 25 percent of cases, widespread absence of overtime payments and wage levels generally 20 percent below the European Union average.

The following national examples from Europe and North America are illustrative:

- In Switzerland, despite an agreement of 1 January 1999 covering all hotel and restaurant employees, HCT workers had average monthly earnings of Sw.frs.3,394 for an effective working week of 42.8 hours, while monthly pay in the economy as a whole averaged Sw.frs.5,000.

- In the United Kingdom, average weekly wages for full-time manual, hotel and catering jobs were £225.80 for men and only £170.80 for women in 1998, while national average wages for manual workers were £328.00 for men and £211.00 for women.
- In New Orleans in the United States, the Hospitality, Hotels and Restaurant Organizing Council (HOTROC) has stated that an average hotel housekeeper earns US$5.48 an hour, which places most hotel workers and their families 20 percent below the federal poverty level. In this connection it should be noted that hotel workers in New Orleans are the only non-unionized hospitality workers in a major United States tourist and convention destination.
- In Canada, average weekly earnings increased by 5 percent in the accommodation sector between 1998 and 1999, but food and beverage earnings lag far behind, having risen by only 1.9 percent, in line with inflation. The average weekly wage in Canada in accommodation is Can$309.14, and in food and beverage Can$221.30. These wages should be viewed against the national average wage of Can$582.85 a week.

Such comparisons do not give a complete picture of the wage structure in the industry. For one thing, comparisons between HCT sector wages established by law or collective agreements and national averages may not fully account for the real wages in those branches where tips or gratuities account for a sizeable proportion of employees' earnings.

These are not always declared for tax purposes, nor are they always known by the employer, and may thus represent a net, tax-free source of income. Secondly, comparisons need to be made with similar occupations of equivalent skill and training levels in other sectors, but the statistical basis for doing so is often lacking. They are taken from the few countries where sufficient information is available.

Changing Forms of Remuneration

Basic wages reflect competitive labour markets, collective agreements and national laws. Variable pay is emerging as a way to reward employees whose performance enhances the success of an establishment. As a strategy, this idea is not yet common in the sector, but it is beginning to take hold. In the United States, Rodeway Inn International, at Orlando, and Motel Properties, Inc. have both developed successful techniques to reward employees above their basic salaries, based on a monthly assessment scheme.

Job and Income Stability and Staff Turnover

Turnover figures vary from region to region within countries, but the overall picture is alarming. In the United States, according to a 1998 study, 21 annual turnover in 1997 was running at 51.7 percent for line-level employees, 11.9 percent for supervisory levels, and 13.5 percent for property managers. The study shows that the turnover rate for the managerial levels is far lower than for line employees. In Asia, rates of around 30 percent annually are quoted, rising to more than 50 percent in Hong Kong, China (possibly owing to the construction of numerous hotels, creating a more competitive labour market). In the United Kingdom, a study carried out by the Institute of Personnel and Development in 1997 found a national turnover rate in the sector of 42 percent, second only to the retail trade, with a rate of 43.5 percent and far in advance of construction, where the rate was 25 percent. In the fast food sector, in both Europe and the United States, turnover rates as high as 300 percent are reported. It should be noted, however, that turnover figures do not separate out non-standard, part-time jobs from full-time posts. Many employees, such as college students, are not interested in permanent positions.

An American Hotel Foundation report puts the cost of replacement of hourly employees at between US$3,000 and US$10,000, while the average figure for restaurant employees is similar, at US$5,000. Many companies equate the cost of losing a trained manager with roughly one year's salary, allowing for the time it takes for the replacement to become fully operational. In the United Kingdom, the 1997 report by the Institute of Personnel and Development estimated the cost of replacing a worker in the hotel and leisure industry at £1,922, and concluded that an average of ten weeks was required for training.

Recent negotiations within the European Union in the context of the employer-driven search for greater flexibility at work raise the prospect of improved conditions for part-time and fixed-term contract workers. The European Trade Union Confederation (ETUC) has made clear its position that if employers require more flexibility, then workers must have better protection.

The Union of Industrial and Employers' Confederations of Europe (UNICE), which represents private-sector employers, has said that employers are prepared to discuss discrimination against agency workers, provided that the unions recognize that temporary work is an integral part of a functioning market. The UNICE has also called for an easing of restrictions to allow shorter contracts and greater flexibility in their renewal. The ETUC has observed that temporary agency work is increasing all over the European Union. It doubled between 1996 and 1998 in Spain, while in France and Germany it increased by 30 percent in three years.

Causes of Turnover

Different reasons for high turnover are cited by employers and employees. Employers' representatives generally consider that turnover in the industry should be attributed to the essentially transient nature of part of the workforce, namely students, young mothers and young people as a whole, as well as to the general difficulty in retaining staff.

Employees, on the other hand, frequently cite low pay as a reason for changing employment, although lack of a career structure and benefits would appear to be of even greater importance. In the United States, for example, even if hotels and restaurants pay US$12.00 an hour, they are in competition with such jobs as bank tellers, and restaurant work retains the stigma of being physical work. Job stability, career prospects and reasonable hours of work are all part of the equation. As long as other jobs offer equal levels of pay, but more advantageous working and employment conditions, the problem of turnover will persist in the hotel and restaurant sector, unless the industry can create equivalent conditions or compensate in other ways. The transparency provided by the Internet will only serve to highlight these factors as they become more widely known.

Measures to Prevent Turnover

In companies where employees are recognized as valued assets and receive the training needed to assume greater responsibility, and where their opinion is sought with regard to operational changes, turnover rates are lower. A study carried out at Purdue University in the United States on the basis of questionnaires sent out to 255 fast food outlets found that establishments which provided a package of benefits to their employees were less affected by turnover. Turnover fell by around 30 percent among employees who could expect scheduled wage increases, paid holidays, health and life insurance and Christmas bonuses.

Prevailing Working Conditions

Working Hours

Many branches of the industry are acknowledged to be particularly arduous in terms of workload and hours of work. In France, where the 35-hour working week is due to come into force for companies with more than 20 employees by 1 January 2001, and for all firms by 1 January 2002, the hotel and restaurant subsectors, which overwhelmingly come within the sphere of family-owned small businesses, regard this legislation with some trepidation. Fifteen years of negotiation were needed to arrive at a national collective agreement for the hotel and restaurant sector in 1997, providing for a working week of 43 hours.

A survey carried out by the European Foundation for the Improvement of Living and Working Conditions covering all 15 European Union countries in 1996 found that 50 percent of hotel and restaurant sector employees worked irregular hours; 80 percent worked two to five Sundays in a month, and 41 percent worked six or more nights monthly. In France, Decorators, a travel agency that is 100 percent electronically operated, has applied the 35-hour legislation in France since 1 June 2000. Teams have been increased by 10 percent to compensate, while the working day has been reduced to 6.8 hours, with seven hours paid. The agency is open from 8 a.m. to 7 p.m., seven days a week, and operates flexibly. This system has been favourably received by staff, who can, for example, choose to work on Sundays and take Wednesdays off in order to care for children.

There is also a rotation of weekend work to ensure a fair distribution of the less social working hours. The tour operator Nouvelles Frontires has reached a different agreement after nine months of negotiation. The company has signed an agreement to increase its staff by 8 percent with the help of state subsidies. Employees will be able to organize their working time according to one of three formulas, namely a four-day week without reduction in pay, a four-and-a-half-day week, or a five-day, 40-hour week yielding 28 extra leave days. The employees must decide on one of the formulas for a period of one year, planned in advance with their supervisors in the services and agencies.

The French fast food sector signed an agreement on 15 April 1999 effectively reducing the working week to 35 hours as of 1 November 1999. This could create between 2,000 and 3,000 new jobs in a sector that employs 80,000 people in France. A national agreement signed on 1 April 1999 also reduced the working week to 35 hours for amusement park employees, with no loss of pay. Moreover, the 35-hour week is being implemented by some employers in the French institutional catering market.

In the United Kingdom, the British Hospitality Association (BHA) claims that the new European Union Working Time Directive restricts working hours although there is no evidence that staff want them restricted. The BHA argues that the 11-hour obligatory break between shifts may cause problems for hotels with receptionists who like to see guests in at night and out in the morning, and for kitchen and restaurant staff serving dinner and breakfast.

Reduction in Workloads

A number of negotiated workload reductions have emerged recently in Europe and North America. In the institutional catering sector of the Netherlands, a recently negotiated national collective agreement provides for a 10 percent annual reduction in workloads based on evaluations at the workplace. Procedures are to be established for handling workload-related grievances, and temporary contracts must now state the actual number of hours worked. The possibility of early retirement at 61 years with 80 percent pay is included in the agreement. A collective agreement ratified by HERE Local 2 in the United States covers 11 hotels in San Francisco. The agreement introduces a doubling of retirement benefits, a reduction in the number of rooms per housekeeper from 15 to 14, and average pay rises of 3.78 percent. It also contains provisions on the specific rights of migrant workers, health coverage, extra personnel for special events and workloads.

Accidents, Violence and Stress at the Workplace

Work-related injuries tend to be more frequent, if generally less serious, in the HCT industry than they are in construction. Almost 50 percent of workplace managers have reported one or more occurrences of work-related illness in the preceding year. Of these, stress is the most common. 30 Violence in the work context is on the increase. The ILO publication "Violence at work" identifies hotel, catering and restaurant staff as likely to experience violence and quotes a recent survey into the extent of violence in pubs in southern England according to which 24 percent of pub licensees felt "highly" at risk and nearly another quarter felt "quite" at risk.

The Challenge of HIV/AIDS at the Workplace

While the chances of contracting or communicating HIV are minimal in the industry, training is needed to assuage personnel fears and make staff aware of the risks that do exist. In terms of employment, the disease may have an impact on three major areas of a business: productivity, employee benefits and morale. The establishment of an HIV policy within an enterprise is therefore a necessity, irrespective of the level of HIV infection in individual countries. In respect of workers who become infected, a number of good practices have come to the fore over recent years. For example, if a worker is HIV-infected, employers should: accept a less than ideal level of performance, as long as minimum standards are met; modify the employee's job description or reassign the employee to a different job; allow more time off for health appointments (with or without pay); allow more sick leave or absenteeism (with or without pay); arrange a more flexible work schedule, or provide for the employee to switch to part-time work, or allow the employee to work from home. Confidentiality of medical information should be ensured, and the UNAIDS recommendations against mandatory HIV testing of staff should be respected.

Subcontracting

As a means of lowering costs, a growing management trend has been to subcontract various services in the industry, such as food and beverages, housekeeping, laundry services, security and valeting. Hotels are increasingly grouping together to employ a common Internet reservation system provider, resulting in a reduction in jobs in the hotels concerned. Hotels are also leasing out their restaurants, particularly in the food and beverage market segment. This implies a severe drop in union membership if the employees of the outsourced companies are non-union members. The New York-New York Casino in Las Vegas in the United States has outsourced virtually all its food and beverage operations to the Ark Restaurants Corporation. There is a differential of around US$6 an hour between the wages paid by Ark and the "Strip Agreement" negotiated by HERE Local 226. HERE therefore regards outsourcing as a means whereby management can impose less favourable conditions on workers by avoiding a collective bargaining agreement. The union calculates that, for Ark to make a profit in this traditionally low- or no-margin operation, they must continue to pay between 25 and 50 percent below union-scale wages.

Non-standard Employment and Working Conditions

The nature of many jobs in the tourism industry creates an atypical employment relationship and special working conditions, such as flexible working time and temporary or part-time work. In addition, there is a general demand by enterprises for greater flexibility in working relations, so as to increase productivity in the face of the growing international competition which is now only a "dot-com away". The 1999 Joint ECF-IUF and HOTREC

Declaration for the promotion of employment in the European hotel and restaurant sector 34 states that, while nonfull- time work can be attractive to employees for a variety of reasons, flexible work organization models should not be introduced simply to suit employers' needs, but must also correspond to employees' wishes. The social partners are called on to examine the possibility of elaborating concepts which combine enterprises' needs for flexibility with workers' needs for security.

Casual Staff

The Swiss trade journal, "Expresso", defines casual workers as those who are employed on an occasional and irregular basis in connection with specific short-term requirements. In Switzerland, the casual worker has the same legal rights as a full- or part-time worker, and the only difference lies in the fact that holidays may be paid in the form of a 10.65 percent supplement to the hourly wage for regimes allowing five weeks' annual holiday, or an 8.33 percent supplement for regimes of four weeks' annual holiday. A similar system prevails in France. A hotel in London has sought to solve the problem of irregular workload peaks by employing university students on a part-time basis for a fixed number of hours annually, in this instance 500 hours, which can be used as required, with students able to exchange hours among themselves according to their individual availability. According to the IUF, the need for labour flexibility has always given rise to problems in respect of maintenance of permanent staffing levels in the hospitality industry, and there is a very high proportion of part-time and casual work compared to other industries. 38 The union notes, however, that the greater the degree of flexibility, the weaker the employer's direct control over labour. Moreover, casual employees are likely to be less committed to the enterprise. Employers, too, are conscious that the casualization of the workforce results in less loyalty to the enterprise and lower skill levels.

Seasonal Variations

In the context of a considerable overall increase in the HCT sector's workforce, seasonal employment and part-time work have also grown substantially. In Austria, there is a 26 percent seasonal variation in employment in the sector; in Spain the figure is 47 percent; in Italy it is more than 50 percent, while in Denmark the number of employees in the sector doubles during the summer season. Part-time work has also been growing faster than full-time employment in the service sector in Australia, where its incidence is relatively high by international standards, particularly among women.

Advantages and Disadvantages of Non-standard Forms of Labour

The 1995 Joint ECF-IUF Declaration on Flexibility of Labour and Organization of Working Time, Part-time Work and the Creation of Jobs, while stating that the creation of full-time jobs is a priority, lists a number of advantages which part-time work may present for both employers and workers. Such employment may correspond to the needs of certain groups of workers – students, parents wishing to accommodate family responsibilities, workers in need of time for training or a flexible transition to retirement through reduced working time. It may also provide a means of reintegration into the labour market for the long-term unemployed. On the other hand, there is the risk that such employment may lead to the creation of a kind of secondary labour market, lacking the same levels of social security cover as a result of minimum hourly thresholds for access to entitlements including training, proportionately lower pay, and the inability of these employees to participate in the collective bargaining process. Moreover, regulatory attempts by governments to create employment by reducing the charges payable on parttime labour can encourage over-reliance on such labour, to the detriment of fulltime jobs.

Measures to Alleviate the Negative Impact of Non-standard Working Arrangements

In Australia, research in 1996 showed that casual workers accounted for over 50 percent of employees in the industry. The unions responded by advocating the replacement of casual jobs with permanent, part-time posts, thus seeking an improvement in, rather than the elimination of, part-time work. 41 The rates of pay received by casual employees remained higher than those paid to permanent part-time workers, but did not include benefits such as paid holidays. Some employees enjoyed the very wide degree of flexibility offered by casual employment, while for employers it presented the advantage of allowing them to dismiss employees without a period of notice. As a result of union activity, some industry agreements were reached, containing an explicit management and union commitment to convert casual hours to permanent, part-time hours, but enforcement has remained limited. These agreements have still not enhanced workers' access to training, and they continue to provide considerable potential for highly irregular working hours.

An example of good practice is provided by the Granada Entertainment and Hotel Group in the United Kingdom, which owns several theme parks, nightclubs and hotels. The group has extended to its part-time employees, who represent 50 percent of the workforce, the same rights and privileges as those enjoyed by full-time employees. Annual performance reviews are carried out for all workers, and the company has introduced formal training for part-time employees to enable them to study for national vocational qualifications.

Another case in point is the Netherlands, where working hours have been made very flexible. Although hotel, restaurant and catering workers may have to work irregular hours, they reportedly have an increasing choice available to them. A law has also recently been passed according to which workers have the right under certain conditions to switch to part-time work should they choose to do so.

In areas where the seasonal element of the trade is particularly marked, and where the hotels or restaurants will only function during a limited period of the year, tourist establishments are obliged to close during the low season, with many of the staff, including hotel and restaurant owners, drawing unemployment benefit. The Scottish winter sports centre at Aviemore has made considerable headway in countering this problem by promoting itself as a centre for "green" tourism and an ideal base from which to explore the surrounding Cairngorm region. The area has undertaken this promotion in partnership with conservation societies to ensure the sustainability of the venture, and much of the business now takes place during the summer months.

Employment Effects of more Recent Forms of Tourism

Cultural Tourism and Ecotourism

The rise of these forms of tourism, in which indigenous peoples also play a role, reflects an interest in other environments, ways of life and cultures. Moreover, it reflects a desire on the part of the tourist for more socially responsible types of tourism, underscoring the idea that some profits should be returned to indigenous peoples in the form of income, and in keeping with environmental concerns.

Ecotourism is a fruitful source of jobs and, if provided with the appropriate means, can provide lasting employment in regions not reached by other industries. Local inhabitants can be employed as guides and rangers, in the lodges or hotels created to deal with the influx of tourists, or as interpreters. Labour is required to build and maintain the infrastructure needed to open up access to the regions in question. The economic benefits to remote communities, if carefully managed and shared fairly among the local people, can be used sensitively to raise educational and living standards without obliterating local culture.

Local populations also have great expertise in the conservation of their own surroundings and may therefore be well employed as experts on the safeguarding of the biodiversity in their regions. Research suggests that ecotourism is growing substantially. A 1996 report by the United States Departments of the Interior and Commerce found that expenditure on wildlife-watching trips rose by 21 percent between 1991 and 1996. The Santa Ana National Wildlife Refuge on the Rio Grande River in the south-western part of the country attracts 100,000 visitors annually and contributes around US$14 million to the local economy each year. The State of Texas has been promoting this type of tourism, having realized that its rare and varied flora and fauna represent a unique natural capital. A task force established to investigate the question defined such tourism as "discretionary travel to natural areas that conserves the environmental, social and cultural values, while generating an economic benefit to the local community".

In Africa, safari tours have existed for many years, but over time negative effects have become apparent, and a more careful approach has been adopted in certain cases. An example is Kenya, where the Masai people were evicted from their traditional lands in 1984 to make way for conservation and safari tourism. As a result, the Masai began poaching and killing the wild animals, in the belief that this would stop tourists coming and they would get their lands back. Negotiation concluded with the Masai people by a Kenyan organization, Porini Ecotourism (in association with a British tour operator), resulted in the Masai receiving a rent for the lease of their land, plus an entry fee for each tourist visitor. In an inspired piece of reconversion, skilled members of the Masai who had been active in tracking and killing wild animals are now engaged as game scouts and guides and, as wildlife watching has grown, poaching has declined. Subsidiary employment effects include jobs in transportation and building and as hotel and catering staff in the many safari lodges in the area. The profits realized by this system are used for the maintenance of boreholes, animal husbandry and education for the Masai. Tourism can thus be seen to work for the local population, both in terms of providing job opportunities and in raising education and training levels.

One of the challenges presented by ecotourism is not just the creation of employment in remote areas, but the offer of higher quality opportunities for indigenous people. In Brazil, local people were initially employed in lower paid, less visible positions in hotels and lodges, since they had little notion of how to deal with tourists. Subsequently, the Brazilian Ministry of Labour, with funds from FAT (the Worker Assistance Fund), established the National Professional Tourism Education Programme. Over the past three years the programme has been used to provide a large body of professionals in various tourism-related activities and is expected to lead to greater numbers of local people being engaged in employment in national parks and reserves.

Similarly, in Uganda, the Budongo Forest Ecotourism Project (BFEP) was started in 1993 with the specific intention of involving the local population in forest conservation. Local communities were included in discussions regarding the planning of the project and encouraged to participate in its development and management. By 1997, 28 local people (eight women and 20 men) were employed by the project. The women work as guides, facilitators and caretakers, and the men perform similar tasks, as well as working as trail cutters. Women are able to sell their craftwork at the tourist sites to supplement their income; six primary schools have received assistance through funds provided by the project, while the local community is provided with a forum in which to resolve its conflicts with the Forest Department.

Negative Effects of Ecotourism

In western Malaysia, the Taman Negara National Park is a privately owned park and resort which can house 260 visitors at a time. The park employs 270 people and 60 percent of the staff in the administrative headquarters are locals, who in 1999 earned about US$120 a month; by comparison, Malaysians living off the land at that time were earning on average about US$40 a month. Despite the positive employment effects, the differences in income between the two groups have led to social tension and driven up boat fares and the cost of everyday goods.

Little of the tourism money goes to the country of destination, while park employees spend almost 90 percent of their income outside the region or on imported goods. Thus local inhabitants, whose culture has been marketed to attract tourists, benefit only to a very limited extent. Indeed, many have taken to illegal hunting and fishing in the park, contrary to the protective regulations established by the park authorities. There is a clear need to establish guidelines and engage local people in dialogue to ensure that the regions and their populations benefit from the tourists' visits.

Adventure Tourism

Activities such as biking, horse riding, trekking, rafting and kayaking, as well as relatively high-risk and more recent sports such as canyoning, are becoming increasingly popular. The Adventure Travel Society, based in Colorado, estimates that the industry expanded by 38 percent between 1991 and 1997, generating

US$220 billion through sales of adventure travel and associated equipment. A number of vocational training institutions – for example, the Nelson Polytechnic in Wellington, New Zealand – are offering courses in adventure tourism, which shows the rising popularity of the field and points to possibilities for employment as accompaniers, monitors and guides. In India also, the Karnataka State Tourism Development Corporation (KTDC) has decided to set up three adventure sports/tourism academies to provide two-year courses to train skilled adventure tourism personnel. The KTDC operates three adventure tour camps near Bangalore and has difficulty finding staff to operate the camps. The training institutions are to be run by private sector partners and adventure tourism companies, but the KTDC plans to arrange tour operator sponsorships for the students, linked to employment following completion of their courses.

Rural or Nature Tourism

The globalization of agriculture markets has placed a strain on certain domestic markets, at the same time as agreements within the World Trade Organization have reduced subsidies to producers and liberalized trade. Farmers in traditionally agrarian areas of Europe have had to seek alternative means of supplementing their income. This may partly explain the rise of rural and nature tourism. In the United Kingdom, it is estimated that 90 percent of all farms provide some form of tourist accommodation. The breakup of farming collectives in countries in transition to a market economy has also encouraged the spread of rural tourism establishments.

The sector remains largely unstructured. It is characterized by large numbers of owner-operators who expand their activities to include the provision of board and lodging. While it may stabilize a precarious financial situation for a population whose income has fallen, its effect in terms of job creation is doubtful. This is not to underestimate its popularity: in 1997, the French public spent a total of 315 million nights in rural vacation areas in France. French rural lodging includes 76,715 hotel rooms, 55,000 beds in vacation villages (*villages de vacances*), 237,558 places in campsites, 41,868 rentable country residences (*gites ruraux*), 1,500 hiking lodges (*gites database*) and 21,466 bed and breakfast rooms. In Italy also, agritourism is seen as a means of providing or supplementing livelihoods, and a list of farms and other establishments providing this service is available from the Italian State Tourist Board. In Cyprus, a plan for the development of such tourism was launched in 1991 and has resulted in the establishment of traditional holiday centres with a capacity of 300 beds.

In this instance, most of these centres remain open throughout the year, although in most countries rural tourism is marked by a strong degree of seasonality. In India, the Karnataka State Tourism Development Corporation has introduced a "bed and breakfast" concept in Coorg and Chikmagalur near Bangalore, where there are very few hotels but many large private residences where house owners could provide paying-guest accommodation. The scheme has proved successful and is to be extended to other parts of the State.

The professicnal part of the sector appears keen to safeguard itself from what might constitute unfair competition, since the type of rural establishments described do not have to meet the same standards as fully fledged hotels. The 1995 Joint ECF-IUF and HOTREC Declaration on tourism in rural areas, while recognizing the decline in agricultural employment and the growing demand for countryside holidays, seeks to protect the hotel industry from any imbalance which might be caused by subsidizing the rural sector. The Declaration stresses that the development of rural tourism "should at all times be market-led rather than grant-led", and that "no form of tourism should be supported to the detriment of another".

Policies to Strengthen the Tourism Sector and the Mployment Effects of such Policies

Regulatory and Deregulatory Measures

The proliferation of regulations in the HCT sector is increasingly a subject of debate in certain regions such as the European Union. In the United Kingdom, one estimate suggests that a small restaurant must comply with 86 Acts of Parliament. In France, where the rule concerning smoking areas in public eating establishments has been poorly applied and, perhaps as a consequence, widely ignored, enforcement of many European Union regulations will be slow, since the premises in which restaurants are installed cannot be brought into line with the required standards so soon. This will inevitably cause problems for many small enterprises, especially those established in old buildings. These will disappear from the sector if the regulations are rigorously implemented, with obvious employment consequences, at least in the short and medium term.

The HOTREC has compiled "200 European Union measures affecting the hotel, restaurant and cafe sector", most of which will be or have already been implemented through national legislation. The industry in the European Union is concerned that they will adversely affect its ability to compete with other countries. United Kingdom employers are expressing concern about the European Working Time Directive, while in France, the more stringent requirements of the 35-hour week are reportedly causing problems for employers. Consequently, the United Kingdom's Ministry for Tourism in September 2000 announced the establishment of a new group to provide far simpler guidelines to regulate the industry. It has also suggested that a task force be established to perform a similar function at European level. Switzerland's Federal Council in January 1997 presented a programme designed to reduce the burden of "red tape" on SMEs. A number of European Union and other OECD countries have already engaged in a deregulatory process.

Taxation of Business in the Hotel, Catering and Tourism Sector

The industry is in favour of ongoing tourism investment and accepts the need for effective taxation. However, large increases in tax on international tourism and travel, which is basically an indirect tax on export earnings, cannot be implemented without an impact on levels of business, and consequently on employment. The globalization of the economy and the ease with which we can now move about the world will only serve to highlight this, as comparative costs of different destinations become apparent through ICT. Recent WTTC figures reveal, however, that between 1994 and 1999, taxes increased in 42 out of 52 destinations, stayed level in two and decreased in eight. The WTTC is of the opinion that industry growth, investment and job creation is most likely to occur in destinations with supportive tax regimes.

The European Union allows a lower rate of value added tax (VAT) on accommodation and certain other tourism and leisure facilities. Ireland chose to lower VAT on accommodation and restaurants in the 1980s, and it is estimated that this led to the creation of 30,000 jobs in the industry. A 1997 study by Deloitte and Touche concluded that reducing VAT in all sectors of the tourism industry would result in the creation of 50,000 jobs. The WTO argues that reductions of this sort, by improving international competitiveness, can also result in higher total tax receipts, rather than the opposite.

Within the European Union, the situation regarding taxation is highly complex, with different rates of VAT and other taxes applying in different countries, and different rates applied within countries depending on the sectors.

A similar situation prevails elsewhere. In India (Tamil Nadu State), a luxury tax of 25 percent has been imposed on hotels with a tariff of more than Rs.1,000, and Tamil Nadu is thus placed at a disadvantage compared to neighbouring States, where taxes of 15 percent or less are applied. Travel agencies offering packages will clearly link up with hotels charging lower taxes.

The industry therefore sees a need for reductions in taxes that are perceived to be damaging productivity, and for harmonization of taxation levels, not only within the European Union, but at international level.

The 1999 Joint ECF-IUF and HOTREC Declaration for the promotion of employment in the European hotel and restaurant sector 61 refers (in section II.2a) to the need for a "level playing field", stating that many countries now competing with the European Union as tourist destinations, particularly the non-European Union Central and Eastern European and Mediterranean countries, "do not pay European Union level VAT, energy taxes, environmental taxes, social charges and the numerous other taxes and charges which burden European enterprises".

Importance of SMEs in the HCT Sector

The last two decades have seen a growing recognition of the important role of small and medium-sized enterprises (SMEs) in employment creation and the promotion of economic growth and development. The general characteristics, potential and problems of SMEs have been a subject of debate within the ILO for many years. A comprehensive discussion on the subject took place at the 72nd Session of the International Labour Conference in 1986, which adopted a resolution concerning the promotion of SMEs. This was followed by more recent discussions on the subject in the context of the promotion of self-employment at the 77th Session of the Conference in 1990 and at several recent regional conferences, including the Eighth African Regional Conference in 1994. Finally, the topic was included on the agenda of the 85th Session of the International Labour Conference in 1997, leading to the adoption in June 1998 of the *Job* Creation in Small and Medium-Sized Enterprises Recommendation, 1998 *(No. 189)*. These debates reflect the extent to which the focus on the enterprise is central to the ILO approach to economic growth, job creation and decent work, an approach exemplified by the In Focus Programme on Boosting Employment through Small Enterprise Development.

SMEs form the majority of enterprises throughout the world in general and in the tourism and hospitality industry in particular. 64 The characteristics of SMEs in the tourism industry include flexibility, direct control of service delivery, personalized and tailor-made service, entrepreneurial activity, strong local character, willingness to cater for special interest groups, employment of family members, flexible timetables and multiskilled personnel.

SMEs play an important role in the European hotel and catering sector. The average number of employees per enterprise ranges from 3.3 to 7.5, except in the United Kingdom, where it can be up to ten.

Support to Small Enterprises

SMEs, because of their fragmented nature, lack opportunities to make economies of scale. They are often operated by non-professionals who lack the marketing skills required to optimize their business opportunities, and they experience difficulties in gaining access to training. The Tourism Conference held from 20 to 22 May 1998 in Llandudno under the United Kingdom's Presidency of the European Union, proposed a ten-point framework for action in support of SMEs in tourism. These recommendations were aimed, among other things, at modernizing the sector in the light of globalization by raising awareness among SMEs of business support systems, information technology and the possibilities open to them in respect of finance, and by providing affordable possibilities for better training for managers/owners and staff.

Governments seek to create an enabling environment for SMEs. In this respect, the move noted previously towards a simplification of the regulations governing the sector is positive, since the high cost, in both time and money, of lengthy administrative procedures raises difficulties for small structures. However, this does not mean that social objectives should be undermined. The European Union High Level Group on Tourism and Employment has called for a Community initiative which "promotes the development of innovative tourist businesses by young entrepreneurs". Large hotel chains are able to establish their own training programmes, often by linking up with public or private education and training establishments. Governments may also provide assistance to SMEs unable to upgrade their employees' skills themselves. One example from the United Kingdom is the Tourism Opportunities Programme (TOPS), which was set up to provide public sector subsidized training. The scheme provides affordable training in areas where individual hotels could not justify creating specialist courses, and may thus benefit from economies of scale.

Large hotel groups such as Accór and Radisson have their own central reservation systems (CRSs) which the public can access via the Internet. While a degree of interactive reservation may come to the SME sector, especially in view of the potential marketing possibilities provided by the World Wide Web, SMEs are for the time being largely dependent on traditional distribution channels. Through their tourist offices, many governments provide networking and marketing services for their hotels and tourist establishments at national or regional level, either free of charge or at a reasonable cost. In France and Spain, tourist offices in larger towns and cities are able to give information about availabilities in establishments within the regions they cover. In the United Kingdom, in the London districts of Greenwich and Islington, the visitor and tourist information centres provide information not only regarding the larger hotels, but also on bed and breakfast establishments in their areas. These centres provide an important support mechanism and marketing tool for very small businesses, which might otherwise remain marginal. The problem of how to classify the levels of service provided in such establishments is another area in which governments could act.

Access to Credit

Finance is a recurring problem for small enterprises. The entrepreneurs concerned may have no professional background or training, and this naturally deters banks. Their financing requirements tend to be small, with consequently higher transaction costs for banks, and such businesses also have a problem finding guaranteed collateral. Many governments intervene by providing interest rate subsidies or guarantees to lending institutions, and some governments, as in India, Indonesia, the Republic of Korea, Malaysia, Pakistan and the Philippines, have imposed minimum quotas on financial institutions for loans to SMEs. Experience has shown, however, that the underlying problem for small entrepreneurs is not the cost of credit, but obtaining access to it via the lending institutions.

Policies Concerning the Informal Sector

According to ILO estimates, the informal sector worldwide employs about 500 million workers. With the process of globalization, the informal sector is gaining importance as a result of its job creation capacity. It generated 80 percent of new jobs in Latin America between 1990 and 1994, while in Africa it was expected to produce 93 percent of new jobs in the 1990s. These employment trends give an idea of the number of workers engaged in unorganized and unprotected jobs, most of them with low income and often poor working conditions.

Since the industry is a labour-intensive sector, the high labour costs may be one reason for recourse to undeclared work in some areas, and employers have criticized governments for failing to integrate informal sector activities into the formal sector. Hotels and restaurants, by providing entry-level employment, play a role in bringing workers from the informal sector into a more formalized labour market, and employers argue that lower labour costs would increase this effect. The ILO National Workshop on the Strategic Approach to Job Creation in the Urban Informal Sector in India has considered a new approach to the informal sector which reflects current thinking in that country. Recent estimates suggest that the informal sector accounts for 90 percent of new jobs in the country. Both employers and workers at the workshop were concerned at the increasing informalization of labour in the economy. One solution to the problem would be to increase the capacity of the sector to offer decent employment, extending social protection as widely as possible to avoid compromising social objectives. This would involve transfers of technology, efforts to increase the informal sector's access to training, credit and markets, and measures to ensure that workers' interests are represented through social dialogue mechanisms.

Vulnerable Groups

The situation of some particularly vulnerable groups of workers is a key issue in view of the technological changes occurring in the hotel and tourism industry. The ILO's *World Employment Report 1998-99*, which deals with national policies in a global context, stressed the need for equity in reform programmes to ensure that vulnerable groups benefit from the processes of globalization in general and from new economic opportunities created by market reforms in particular. Tourism employment is an alternative to traditional and more rigorous work, such as agriculture or fishing, and provides both men and women with greater occupational choices.

Young People

Young people who are marginalized are generally poor, with little education and training. Migration also tends to exacerbate the process of marginalization. Eighty-five percent of young people live in developing countries, and that proportion is expected to increase to about 89 percent by 2020. UNESCO estimates that approximately 96 million young women and 57 million young men are illiterate, the majority in developing countries. AIDS also increases the vulnerability of the young: the Joint United Nations Programme on HIV/AIDS (UNAIDS) notes that over a third of the 30 million people with the HIV infection or full-blown AIDS are aged between 10 and 24 years. The number of younger people employed in formal sector tourism, either as "apprentices" in fast-food chains such as McDonalds and Pizza Hut or as casual workers in occasional or seasonal employment in catering, is also growing rapidly. These types of labour have raised concerns regarding contraventions of labour regulations such as those concerning the minimum legal working age. Research into the Australian youth labour market shows that the impact of labour market deregulation on young workers in the hospitality industry has caused increased income insecurity, wage polarization and deteriorating conditions of employment. Full-time permanent employment is being replaced by part-time and casual work, and average weekly earnings for teenagers in full-time employment have fallen compared to those of young and older adults.

Women

ILO estimates dating back to 1983 indicated that a third of the global workforce in tourism was made up of women. According to more recent estimates, the proportion of women in the tourism industry (excluding the informal sector) has risen to 46 percent, while in catering and accommodation they represent over 90 percent of all employees. They occupy the lower levels of the occupational structure in the tourism labour market, with few career development opportunities and low levels of remuneration (some estimates suggest that wages for women are up to 20 percent lower than those for men). The greater incidence of unemployment among women is attributed to their low skill levels and their low social status in many poor countries. They also tend to be the first affected when labour retrenchment occurs as a result of recession or adjustment to new technology. It should also be noted that the majority of workers in subcontracted, temporary, casual or part-time employment are women. For differences in remuneration between men and women.

Child Labour

Child labour is a matter of grave concern, robbing children of their childhood, stunting their growth and hindering the development of their countries. An estimated 13-19 million children and young people below 18 years of age (10-15 percent of all employees in tourism) are employed in the industry worldwide. Child labour in tourism is common in both developing and in developed countries. Many boys and girls below 12 years of age are engaged in small business activities related to hotels and restaurants, the entertainment sector or the souvenir trade, often as porters or street or beach vendors. They are frequently subjected to harsh working and employment conditions.

It is estimated that about 2 million children throughout the world are subjected to commercial sexual exploitation and thus exposed to such concomitant risks as HIV infection. Tourism must bear its share of responsibility for this trade. There are many factors which can drive families and children away from their homes towards poles of tourist attraction in city centres or coastal regions. Those factors include: civil or national conflicts; ethnic rivalries; family breakdown; excessive urbanization which aggravates overcrowding and creates a range of social ills; diminishing agricultural resources; and other severe economic hardships, such as rising unemployment, national financial crises, and cutbacks in subsidies or other measures introduced under structural adjustment programmes. Child refugees from Somalia and Rwanda are exploited in a number of ways on the beaches of Mombasa. Active recruitment and trafficking agents are a factor in all this, but the lure of consumerism and its images cannot be ignored. These are all underlying reasons which help to explain why children and young people are driven into exploitative employment in the tourism industry, or, worse still, in the sex trade, which operates very lucratively in the tourist centres of Asia, Africa, Latin America, the Caribbean, and the transition countries.

Child Sex Tourism

The sexual exploitation of children of both sexes, as practised through child prostitution and child pornography, forms a sometimes hidden part of the overall commercial sex sector. Although a worldwide phenomenon, it is more prevalent in Asia than eisewhere. In the Philippines, frequently quoted estimates of the number of children involved range from 30,000 to 60,000; a very recent report quotes the figure of 75,000.

The United Nations has defined child sex tourism as "tourism organized with the primary purpose of facilitating the effecting of a commercial sexual relationship with a child". Certain holiday destinations are now frequented by paedophiles. At national level, pimps, taxi drivers, tour operators (by organizing package sex tours), hotel staff, brothel owners and entertainment establishments all work together to satisfy foreign tourists' demand for prostitutes. At the international level, agents disseminate information about particular resorts where such practices are commonplace.

Increasing concern over the appalling conditions of child labour have led to the adoption of new international instruments and action plans by the international community. In 1999, the International Labour Conference unanimously adopted the Worst Forms of Child Labour Convention, and Recommendation No. 190. These instruments declare "the use, procuring or offering of a child for prostitution, for the production of pornography or for pornographic performances" to be one of the worst forms of child labour, and urge ILO member States to take immediate and effective action to prohibit and eliminate it as a matter of priority. The pace of ratification of Convention No. 182 is the fastest in ILO history, with 41 ratifications in just over 16 months.

The quest for improved child protection can also be measured by the worldwide concern about child labour that has been expressed in a number of international forums. Among these are: the Stockholm World Congress against Commercial Sexual Exploitation of Children, 1996; the European Meeting on the International Dimension of Sexual Exploitation of Children, held in Madrid, 1998; the European Meeting of the Main Partners in the Fight against Child Sex Tourism, held in Brussels, 1998; and the UNESCO Expert Meeting on Sexual Abuse of Children, Child Pornography and Paedophilia on the Internet, held in Paris in January 1999. The Global Report on the international dimensions of sexual exploitation of children, which is a follow-up of the Stockholm World Congress, includes recommendations which cover a wide range of measures to protect children from sexual exploitation and ensure that their abusers are properly prosecuted and convicted anywhere in the world. UNICEF has presented a study on extraterritorial criminal laws against child sexual exploitation which includes a series of recommendations on ways of stopping the international market for sex tourists and paedophiles who travel to other countries to exploit children sexually. The Stockholm World Congress is scheduled to be followed by the second of its type in December 2001 in Yokohama, Japan.

With regard to specific action-oriented initiatives originating from the tourism industry itself, IH&RA participates in a task force against child sex tourism coordinated by the World Tourism Organization along with other trade association partners such as the Universal Federation of Travel Agents' Associations (UFTAA), the International Air Transport Association (IATA) and non-governmental organizations such as ECPAT (End Child Prostitution, Pornography and Trafficking).

Apart from setting up its own task force in 1996 to confront the problem of child labour and running an awareness-raising campaign which provides guidelines on how operators and associations can combat child sex tourism, IH&RA is also involved in the work on a code of conduct for the protection of children against commercial sexual exploitation, initiated by ECPAT Sweden and a number of Swedish tour operators along with the partners mentioned above.

The Youth Career Development Programme launched jointly by the Singapore-based Pan-Pacific Hotels and Resorts Group and UNICEF in 1995 is another commendable initiative. This 20-week programme sets as its objective the provision of basic skills in the hospitality industry and long-term social and economic security for young girls exposed to the risk of commercial sexual exploitation. Trade unions have also undertaken action against child sex tourism. The IUF has drawn up a model collective agreement aimed at preventing child sex tourism for use by its affiliated organizations in the tourism industry.

Migrant Labour

The impact of international migrant flows on the tourism labour market of receiving countries is another important issue, whether it concerns daily commuters, seasonal workers or permanent migrants. The majority of them are drawn into lower paid, informal or casual employment in services. Although many migrant workers stay for a number of years, they often remain at low skill levels compared to local workers. Their social status is often equivalent to ethnic minorities, another group strongly over-represented in the HCT sector. In Austria between 1970 and 1995, there was a marked increase in migrant labour employed in hotels and restaurants as compared to other sectors of the economy, but stricter immigration laws in the mid-1990s led to a reduction of new entries. In 1996, the percentage of foreign workers in hotels and restaurants was 51.2 percent in Switzerland and 30.9 percent in Germany.

In Spain, the coastal resorts employ a large number of illegal immigrants. A comparative study of hotel employment and employee development in Finland, Spain, the United Kingdom and Bulgaria suggests that increasingly global tourism markets and the more permeable national and labour market boundaries resulting from economic, political and social integration in Europe have led to a growth in numbers of transient workers and increasingly elastic labour market migration – mainly inwards to the United Kingdom (from Europe and globally) and Finland (from Russia), and mainly outwards from Spain and Bulgaria. In Canada, the labour force in the accommodation sector has historically come from marginalized segments of the labour market, including immigrants. In the hotel sector, there has been a gradual shift towards the employment of newer immigrant groups.

In Germany, McDonalds employs a large number of immigrants, mainly from the former Eastern Bloc, and others who are disadvantaged on the labour maıket owing to language problems and lack of recognition for previous qualifications. In Denmark, the participation of immigrants in the tourism labour market is increasing markedly. From 1980 to 1995, the proportion of immigrants in the tourism workforce increased from 4.9 percent to 7.6 percent. More than 12 percent of all foreigners active in the Danish labour market are employees or business owners in the hotel and restaurant sector, and in 1995, 16.7 percent of immigrants active in tourism were running their own enterprise. Danish employees in tourism enjoy relatively better employment conditions than their immigrant counterparts, who have lower job status, lower earnings, and more family responsibilities. Danish workers in part-time employment are predominantly women, whereas the foreigners are mostly men. Turnover is high for both Danes and immigrants of comparable status, but Danes leaving the sector are absorbed in other sectors while immigrants more often face unemployment or are forced to set up their own enterprises.

Undeclared Labour

The hotel, restaurant and catering sector remains an area in which use is frequently made of undeclared labour. In some countries, this may involve the clandestine employment of illegal foreigners who are willing to accept less advantageous conditions of employment than nationals. It may also take the form of employees being declared as working for a certain limited number of hours while actually working longer hours and receiving supplementary payments in cash, thus enabling both employer and employee to avoid payment of a proportion of social insurance contributions. Undeclared labour is employed mainly in small enterprises where cash is available outside the official accounts. In Switzerland, new legislation has been introduced whereby employers run the risk of imprisonment of up to one year and a fine of up to Sw.frs.500,000 for infractions involving undeclared labour, with more severe sanctions in cases of recurrent contraventions.

3

Human Resource in Tourism

The traditional constraints of the hotel, catering and tourism industry – long, antisocial working hours, low pay, unstable, seasonal employment, low job status, etc. – make employment within the industry appear unattractive to many. A study carried out in 1996 in Germany found that employment in the hotel and catering trade was not the first choice for nine out of ten employees, while only one employee in seven was satisfied with the trade as a choice of career. Nevertheless, the industry does attract some people either on a short-term basis or for a long-term career.

The immediate and most obvious consequences of such a situation are the difficulty of recruiting suitable staff and high staff turnover; both these effects are costly to the industry. There is therefore a perceived need for human resource development, to raise the profile of the industry, increase productivity and provide decent, sustainable employment within the sector.

Estimating Labour Productivity

A wide range of technological developments in service in hotels may be affecting productivity. Integrated management systems are enabling hotel companies to computerize day-to-day reception operations. Clients are thus able to make their own reservations via the Internet, while electronic in-room installations make it possible to settle accounts from the hotel room. This technology will also make it possible to monitor the productivity of personnel, while new techniques in food preparation and storage are reducing the skills needed in the kitchen and the time required for food preparation. 1 Hotels are therefore seeking new ways to measure service delivery that take into account customer satisfaction and return visits, rather than sticking to a narrow "input/output" system.

In Europe, tourist-related activities account on average for 5.5 percent of GDP in all European Union Member States and for a total of 9 million employees, representing 6 percent of the total workforce. The precise percentages vary from country to country. According to WTTC simulated figures, the tourism industry's labour force represents about 3 percent of the world's total labour force and produces about 4 percent of total world GDP. The industry can therefore not be regarded as labour intensive throughout.

The most striking thing to note regarding labour productivity in the different regions is the gap between Europe's average of about US$47,000 per employee and the overall average of US$22,000.

The performance of the Caribbean (around US$28,000) is also impressively higher than average. In the hotel industry in developing countries there may be on average up to three people employed for each hotel bed, while in developed countries the inverse is true, with one person employed for up to three or even four hotel beds. However, figures of this sort can be affected by the range of services provided by a hotel: an establishment surrounded by a leisure complex, health resort or spa will naturally employ more ancillary workers. Labour productivity in hotels has increased over the last ten years by about 1 percent per year. In the United States, the number of employees per 100 hotel rooms sold has declined from 81 in 1986 to 75 in 1997.

The same productivity growth applies to the entire HCT sector whose GDP, according to WTTC simulated figures, has been growing by about 3 percent per year, whilst employment in the industry has grown by only about 2 percent per year. Labour productivity in restaurants is hard to measure. Since only 50-60 percent of all restaurant employees worldwide are full-time workers, the information available hardly allows us to establish absolute productivity ratios.

New Forms of Work Organization

Flexible Work

The First World Travel and Tourism Summit, held in 1977 in Vilamoura, Portugal, recognized that travel and tourism create an unparalleled number of entry-level jobs for young people and women and provides part-time or seasonal employment for people seeking flexible working arrangements.

The Summit called for the reduction of rigid practices in labour markets to encourage greater staff mobility, productivity and innovation in a progressive employment environment, with emphasis on a flexible market economy, avoiding protectionist regulation.

The Conclusions and Recommendations of the European Union's High Level Group on Tourism and Employment 4 drew attention to the fact that notable adjustments were taking place in European tourism, that these were critical to its competitiveness, and that they would lead to important changes in the tourism labour market. Those are: a refocusing of core competencies; a deskilling of operational tasks in some sub-branches; upgrading of skills and specializations, in particular in large enterprises and tourist organizations and in complementary services; and the creation of new professional profiles to meet tourists' needs and preferences.

The document draws attention to a tendency within the industry to transfer work operations from traditional core sectors to ancillary service suppliers. A positive example of flexibility is provided by the Sheraton-Denver West Hotel in the United States, where two experienced sales managers share one full-time job, thus enabling the company to benefit from the energy and experience of two persons for the price of one. In this instance, both managers wanted to work part time to accommodate their personal and family needs. The arrangement was particularly effective, since both managers were in continual contact. Job-sharing opportunities of this kind will be even more viable in the future, as information becomes more comprehensively shared and more easily transmitted.

Seasonal Employment

One opportunity which has been insufficiently investigated is the possibility of using the inter-season period as a time for training to impart new skills, guaranteeing re-employment of qualified staff in successive seasons so as to retain their services. A hotel located in Savonlinna (South-Savo, Finland), a city famous for its summer opera festivals, has adopted this approach. To deal with the multicultural and demanding clientele drawn by the summer festival, the hotel pays its core staff to attend off-season training courses in language skills, knowledge of food and wine and leadership skills. Employee development is seen not as a cost but as an investment which pays good returns during the summer season.

Multiskilling

The employers argue that one way to create sustainable, realistic employment in the industry is to implement a policy of "multiskilling". This is also viewed as a means of reducing the problems of recruitment. Multiskilling has always been practised in small enterprises, but it is only recently that particular attention has been paid to it. As demand for general competencies in small enterprises as well as in major hotel and restaurant chains has grown, and as appropriate means of training for these competencies have been developed, awareness has grown of the importance of multiskilling in that segment. One person fulfilling several roles at different times of the day combines the tasks of several (part-time) jobs into one job. Multiskilling is also seen as a way to create or preserve a number of full-time jobs, as opposed to part-time jobs, since the tasks may be performed at any time of the day. Instead of employing specialists on a less than full-time basis, employees are trained to perform the tasks of several specialists, often supported by facilitating technology. In Finland, a relatively smali hotel has adopted a "multitask" policy. All its employees must be willing to perform any of the tasks that are necessary to operate the hotel.

When hiring staff, the hotel manager gives precedence to "right personality" over all other criteria. Some workers left when this decision was taken which suggests that the approach is not universally appealing to employees. According to the CBI, "... skills flexibility is indispensable for functional flexibility. It requires a strong basic education system and a commitment on the part of employers and employees to the acquisition of new and transferable skills. It helps maintain high employability and reduces frictional unemployment associated with skills mismatch". The IUF, on the other hand, considers that such multiskilling may have the effect of devaluing specific skills, since the flexible worker, as viewed by the employer, has no specialized skills or job qualifications, and performing a variety of tasks requires a lower level of knowledge for each of them. The highly skilled, and consequently better remunerated, specialist worker may become a thing of the past. However, the unions also concede that an employee able to perform a variety of tasks is more valuable to an employer and should be remunerated accordingly.

New Management Methods

Corporate organizations are downsizing and restructuring, which means that they are cutting back on layers of management. This means that less direction is being imparted to employees, who are more frequently required to accept a greater degree of responsibility and accountability. Increased use of technology in the workplace also means an added responsibility for individual workers. It is estimated that the "knowledge revolution", by providing clear information via the Internet on all the industry's tangible elements (illustrations of accommodation and hotel facilities) will make the intangible elements (those imparted by personal contact and service) all the more important. Lower levels of staff will be empowered to act autonomously. Command and control structures are thus largely giving way to a participatory teamwork approach. Human resources trained to fit in with new working methods will have to be regarded as an asset in which investment must be made, rather than merely as a cost, or employees will seek employment elsewhere. Management is developing ways in which to attract and retain employees.

The advent of new technology will not stop the industry from being a supplier of entry-level jobs; clearly, a large number of routine jobs will continue to exist. However, the question of staff retention will remain a management problem. Information technology will make potential entrants to the industry more aware of the possibilities available, compounding the problem for the industry. In order to retain staff, certain companies have already set up an incentive system. McDonalds introduced a broad-based stock ownership programme in 1995 to improve staff morale and productivity, while in Europe, one major hotel chain has established the CHAMPS reward programme, in which employees earn points for cleanliness, hospitality, accuracy, product quality and speed. These points can be used to buy catalogue merchandise.

Career Development

Truly structured careers, in which workers have genuine prospects of career development, are not numerous in the hotel, tourism and catering sector, and efforts to retain employees through incentives or promotion are the exception rather than the rule. Not only do people tend to "pass through" the sector, but research has shown that it is often the most talented who leave, since they are the most confident of finding other employment, while the less confident stay for fear of becoming unemployed. However, for many young people the industry is an entry point to the world of work. It brings workers into direct contact with the public and can provide opportunities for travel. Moreover, for young people, the provision of food and lodging – a common practice in the industry – facilitates entry into active adult life. These factors combine to make tourism a major motor for the social and professional integration of the young.

New and Changing Occupational Profiles

With the advent of new technologies and an increasingly discerning public able to keep informed through the Internet, the hotel sector is being forced to widen its sphere of action beyond the traditional provision of food and accommodation. In the pursuit of improving the intangibles, major hotel chains are seeking to provide more services, both in response to customers' needs and in an effort to provide an "experience" rather than simple lodging. For example, the French Accor Group has expanded into travel agency services, car hire, casinos and on-board train services, while other groups have established connections with sectors that are indirectly linked to tourism, such as insurance, travel articles and health and beauty services. The range of services now expected by customers naturally requires an upgrading of skills among front-desk staff, who will for the most part be required to administer these services. This will call for motivated personnel with excellent social skills and an understanding of what people want.

Advances in computer technology allow far more rapid and detailed generation of information on quality and economic performance. Hotel managers will thus be called on to react more quickly, to analyse situations and take appropriate decisions. The wider range of services on offer will also call for greater marketing skills than were previously necessary. In large hotels and hotel chains this is resulting in the creation of posts which are new to the industry, but which already exist in other fields, such as budget analysis and management accounting expert, quality manager, yield manager, technical and computer services manager. With greater emphasis being placed on environmental protection, there is also an increasing need for experts on the environmental impact and planning of tourism development. Similarly, greater concern over food safety is creating a growing need for food safety and health experts. As the hotel sphere increasingly includes services catering for customers' entertainment needs, sports and games specialists as well as specialized tour guides are opening up as careers in the tourism sector.

Measures to Promote Career Building in the Enterprise

New divisions of labour and changes in the nature of jobs within the tourism sector mean that the industry is employing an increasingly varied range of employees. However, although tourism is a diverse sector which can provide many working opportunities for a wide range of skills, there is a shift within Europe away from specific skills towards broader, more generic competencies. Good practice in training is largely limited to large hotel chains, and small, individual enterprises tend to rely on training given "on the job". According to research in Spain, managers of three-star hotels recognized that older workers rarely had any of the formal training required to deal with a more sophisticated clientele, and younger workers lacked industry-specific practical skills. However, they were generally reluctant or unable to invest in training, on the grounds that the cost could not be sustained by their operations. The key training needs established by employers and trade unions are food safety, IT, environmental awareness and foreign language skills.

The industry provides few post-experience training or retraining opportunities, and, indeed, commitment by the private sector to human resource development appears slight, especially where such development lies beyond their immediate operational needs: "European companies, especially smaller businesses, provide little by way of financial and practical support for human resource development within the wider educational and training framework." Within the multinational hotel industry, however, there is a trend towards investment in education, training and development, to meet the need for a higher level of customer-oriented service. The Radisson Hotel Group acknowledges that the success of the company depends on the knowledge, skills, abilities, motivation and dedication of its employees, and consequently has a well-developed internal training system, with links to outside training establishments as well, to which 0.4 percent of each hotel's total revenue is dedicated.

Through the Radisson SAS climate analysis system, outstanding efforts and exceptional results, both individual and on a team basis, are rewarded through local incentive schemes. The training emphasis is shifting towards continuous learning and increasing the potential of individual employees. A total of 515 employees were trained in 11 different areas in the Radisson SAS Management School in 1999, with specific training in business finance, revenue management, euro handling and business planning. Efforts have been made by the enterprise to establish relations with European and American hotel schools, so that a steady flow of students takes up internships at a Radisson hotel. The Per-Axel Brommesson Scholarship enables four talented employees a year to develop management skills through professional development programmes at institutions such as Cornell University, and other business schools.

In order to bring the training provided by formal education institutions into harmony with the requirements of the everyday operation of the trade, the industry has entered into partnership with teaching establishments, to ensure that the content of their courses is relevant to work in the sector, and to offer students, through that linkage, practical experience in all fields. In the United States in 1996, the Hospitality Business Alliance (HBA) was formed between the National Restaurant Association and the American Hotel and Motel Association to create a school-tocareer programme. Worksite experience is an integral element of the training. During the school year, students work between 15 and 20 hours a week in the enterprise, gaining experience in front-desk operations, housekeeping, room service, safety and health, reservations, sales and marketing and convention services. The system has grown from involving three high schools in 1997 to 600 high schools in 1999, covering 25 States and 11,000 students.

One hotel group in the United Kingdom noted a training gap which was preventing the company's (multi-)unit managers, whose role is a largely implementational one, from progressing to a more strategic role within the enterprise. The company's human resource department has organized strategic management development schemes at a number of leading business schools in the United Kingdom and the United States. The courses are designed to expose area managers to the strategic concepts of operational management, including corporate governance, finance, marketing and human resource strategy. This move to supply appropriate training is appreciated by unit managers aspiring to strategic policy-creative posts.

A number of hotel chains have introduced schemes to enhance careers within their structures, with a view to reducing staff turnover. Choice Hotels International in the United States analysed the requirements for its senior executives on the basis of suitable existing competency models, then assessed the competencies of current top executives and compared these with the competencies needed for the future. This enables the company to carry out annual readiness assessments and to establish a genuine career structure within the group, thus avoiding the disruption and expense of replacing executive staff. A further example is provided by Motel 6, which has established an HRD approach whereby every employee is eligible to become a manager, via a three-tier training scheme. By early 1998 this system had allowed around 300 Motel 6 employees to reach the grade of general managers, thereby helping to fill a need for qualified managers by providing employee training and the basis of a career structure.

Developing Language Skills

An increasingly culturally diverse clientele has necessitated specialist training in the field of knowledge building for staff. ITT Sheraton operates a number of resort hotels in the Hawaiian islands, where the presence of Japanese clients has encouraged the creation of Japanese language and culture courses. This initiative has resulted in a significant increase in the number of Japanese guests frequenting the hotels, while the courses themselves have become problem-solving sessions with staff. In 1992, the Four Seasons Hotel and Resort developed the Self-Access Learning Centre in Indonesia, where the company was opening a new resort, to teach English to locally recruited staff. The courses were designed to take account of the fact that around 80 percent of the staff had no more than primary-school education. The centre now teaches French and Japanese as well as Bahasa Indonesia. Employees are rewarded as they complete each of the five levels of the course with bonuses ranging from Rps.100,000 to Rps.250,000 (about $8-20), and a certificate of achievement. Turnover at the resort is low, at 4-6 percent.

Career Enhancement through Increased Employee Responsibility

The Ritz-Carlton Company has identified the empowerment of individual staff members as a way to retain staff through increased job satisfaction. Employees were invited to take on certain management duties: the front-office employees, for example, were invited to take over the role of the front-office manager. As an incentive, the hotel proposed dividing half of the savings obtained through the elimination of the post among the employees who had taken on the duties (about $1.00 each an hour). The replaced staff members were not sacked, but redistributed elsewhere in the company. At another hotel, a system of self-directed housekeeping teams was established and responsibility given to the teams for choosing their own work areas, evaluating room quality and conducting room inspections; this has increased the staff retention rate and morale among room attendants. 16 In 1993, Accor launched a three-year programme to "re-engineer" the structure of Sofitel North America. The programme was designed to empower employees to make decisions to benefit guests, and called for volunteers eager to make improvements in services provided by the hotels. Since suggestions for improvements and alterations were now originating from the employees, peer resistance within each department was minimal: a culture of trust and communication was established. The result has been an increase not only in customer satisfaction, but in employee satisfaction as well. Staff turnover fell from 58 percent in 1993 to 39 percent in 1998, below the industry average.

Among the reasons frequently cited for reluctance to taking up employment in the hotel, tourism and catering trade, lack of promotion possibilities features prominently. The broad pyramid of the hierarchy within the industry renders interpretation of the word "career" difficult. While careers are possible in the sector, and it is theoretically possible to progress from waiter to managing director of a major hotel chain, the increasingly flat management structures can only make this increasingly difficult. On the other hand, systems designed to reward staff financially for their performance, with the aim of reducing staff turnover and encouraging a feeling of "belonging" to the enterprise, are not yet accepted by all staff, and vertical career aspirations are still widespread. Modern-minded employers trust that job satisfaction is tending to shift away from hierarchical feelings. Bonuses to enhance job satisfaction can be awarded (and sometimes withdrawn) at any time, according to individual or collective performance.

Tourism Education and Training

Recognizing the need for Tourism Education and Training

Employers maintain that many enterprises, especially SMEs, cannot pay wages commensurate with formal training and recognized qualifications. Others argue that the greater productivity made possible by training will make higher wages possible. In general, many of the operational activities in the industry require learning on the job, rather than formal training, and managers frequently state their preference for recruitment on the basis of personality rather than formal qualifications. More than 60 percent of operational staff in Germany and more than half the labour force in Austria have had no formal training. The industry displays a reluctance to give formal recognition to acquired skills, and this may reflect a wish to avoid claims for higher wages and prevent undesired mobility. On the other hand, a recent study also suggests that practical training and experience is more highly valued in the countries covered than formal, accredited training qualifications. Moreover, high staff turnover in the industry makes returns on training investment hard to evaluate. Employees, who may not wish to develop a career in the industry or may be discouraged by poor scholastic performance, also avoid measurement by public standards.

At middle management level and higher, however, tourism education is a formal requirement. In Canada, it is estimated that more than one-third of jobs in hotels require post-secondary education, including language proficiency, but a Brazilian study shows that only 12 percent of hotel and restaurant staff have completed secondary school. Tourism-related degree programmes have been slow to acquire recognition as a truly academic discipline although, given the increasing social and economic importance of tourism, a sound knowledge of its economic, social, cultural, environmental and political dimensions is essential. This is particularly the case in countries, including developing countries, where tourism is growing rapidly. In Europe, tourism training is seen as a means of boosting employment and recouping Europe's dwindling market share in the industry.

New Skill Requirements

In the Rhone-Alpes region of France, 7,000 new hotel and restaurant workers are required. Half the posts do not match formal training schemes. The bipartite committee on vocational training is therefore proposing that graduates acquire additional certificates to become waiters or wine-cellar specialists, as well as cooks, and is considering replacing the certification system with a system listing a variety of competencies. Given the higher customer expectations of quality in a one-to-one relationship with the service personnel, an important part of the required skills concerns personal behaviour and communication, as opposed to specialized operational skills. The new skill requirements have an undeniable vertical element. The joint vocational training committee in Rhône-Alpes therefore recommends recruiting waiters with higher school qualifications (baccalaureate). However, workers with that level of education rarely seek employment as waiters.

More complex workplaces have brought about a shift in training concerns from operational or vocational skills to personal and social skills. Operational skills are still required, but are increasingly focused on technological innovation. A capacity to learn and develop activities, and to assimilate all elements of a complex process, and effective communication skills, including negotiation in cases of conflict, are among the skills needed to enable today's worker to attain the necessary autonomy at work. This presents a challenge for training institutions geared towards operational skills, rather than "soft" skills.

New technical skills which need to be acquired by line-level employees include: deeper and more up-to-date knowledge of materials and production processes; knowledge of computer programs and other new technologies employed in kitchens and the concomitant new working methods; awareness of safety and health issues, an understanding of the house "business culture"; and an ability to impart an increasingly broad range of information to customers. Language knowledge and a developed inter-cultural sensitivity are key skills for tourism personnel who have direct contact with customers.

Management-level requirements mirror the qualities listed above, but also embrace a new approach to human resource management and development. Enterprises are espousing a philosophy by which workers receiving "good service" from their superiors are more likely to provide "good service" to customers.

Another important area of innovation and emphasis for management training is quicker response to – or anticipation of– market developments. This requirement is nothing new for top chain hotel managers, but it is new for many managers of smaller units and for department chiefs or supervisory-level managers. Adjusting in an autonomous way and developing innovative strategies require a capacity to generate the necessary flux of market information, and consequently also the ability to manipulate computer programmes. This marks a significant departure from the traditional picture of the independent hotel manager as "a jack of all trades" who does not work within budgets or performance targets.

The Importance of Continuous Training

Formally structured initial or primary training, including apprenticeships with practical and technical schooling, seems less adapted to the new "soft" skill requirements of today's industry than continuous training, and current thinking holds that it might be restricted to a minimal, multisector learning platform to raise the employability of young people and their mobility between different sectors. Continuous training, which has the advantage that it may be used to react quickly to changing circumstances, is being directed towards imparting the new skills.

Continuous training in the industry is rare, and courses are insufficient in number and in quality. Spain has one of the most generous publicly financed continuous training schemes, under which in 1997 about 17 percent of the 800,000 workers in the sector participated on average in one week's training. Elsewhere, this figure hardly exceeds a few percent. A survey carried out in all 15 member countries of the European Union in 1996 showed that 86 percent of all employees in the hotel and restaurant trade had never received any further training.

Learning for Competencies

Exchanging the concepts of skills, capacities and qualification for that of competencies is consonant with the idea of the enterprise as a learning organization in which personnel have enhanced strategic and problem-solving capacities at all levels. Competencies are described in terms of the results to be achieved, whereas earlier methodologies prescribed tasks, abilities and desired attitudes, leaving the responsibility for the result to the hierarchy.

To promote the new concept, the European Working Group on improving training in the tourism industry" convened by the European Commission recommends that research should be undertaken into ways to develop individuals' capacity to make full use of general, technical and personal skills as well as the "soft skills" needed to make use of the other skills, and into how the enterprise can engage and combine the competencies of individuals in an organic manner.

The concept of competencies and their standardization and certification can more easily be introduced where training schemes are flexible. Modular training has always been the basis of training systems in countries where no neat distinction was made between initial training and continuous training. Courses of varying duration, institutional backing, and funding modalities were extended to students of all ages.

The new concept of competencies can therefore be introduced speedily to satisfy an increasing need for certification arising from more flexible employment relationships.

Training systems in Costa Rica, the Dominican Republic and Mexico now provide standards for competencies in the hotel, restaurant and tourism sector. Whilst employers offer "earning with learning" to encourage multiskilling, i.e. each acquired competency leads to an increment in salary, trade unions observe that the acquisition of various competencies by workers who occupy jobs outside conventional job classifications tends not to be remunerated appropriately.

Bargaining for appropriate remuneration is more difficult where qualifications are diffuse and do not fit into any pre-established scheme. Moreover, bargaining collectively can hardly take account of all possible individual skill combinations. Indeed continuous training has been far less subject to social dialogue than has initial training. Where training for competencies has been introduced, standardization and certification of acquired skills are therefore essential.

Certification

Globalization of the travel and tourism industry and the increased use of e-commerce require a common international understanding and certification of core skills in order to facilitate distance business transactions and assure buyers and sellers that the services they deal with meet certain standards anchored in the qualifications of the labour force. The competitiveness of small tourism enterprises will increasingly depend on the credibility and reliability of the services they can offer. Hotel and restaurant management training provided by colleges and universities is quite transparent even across national borders, but for operational level workers it is often developed by industry associations of the different sectors involved, and it is difficult to avoid overlapping even at the national level.

In recent years, the certification of skills has also been debated as a means of improving the functioning, transparency and permeability of local and national labour markets. Greater workers' mobility between different employers, seasonal locations and ultimately across borders would enhance human resources allocation and create benefits for all players in the sector. On the other hand, there could be immediate disadvantages for some. Increased mobility of workers would counteract efforts made by employers to promote in-house human resources development, as the training and incentives provided would not necessarily pay off within the enterprise. Where elaborate initial training systems exist, they are regarded by trade unions as an acquired right. Certification of skills is therefore not endorsed as a substitute for formal initial training (where it exists), but only as a new way of presenting its results.

Greater international recognition of certification is needed where economic integration creates greater mobility within the labour market. In Latin America, an ILO project in the 1990s assisted nine countries on an inventory of qualifications with a view to agreeing on a common classification at a later stage. The European sectoral social partners are considering a proposal to make the description of acquired skills compatible between the European Union countries. The ECF-IUF and HOTREC are examining the possibility of implementing a "European qualifications passport" for the hotel and restaurant sector. Objections have been voiced on the grounds that certified skills for migrant workers might lead to higher wage claims; however, a qualifications passport could also help employers to find and recruit the right personnel much more easily.

Providers of Continuous Education and Training

There is a very wide range of private, public and semi-public institutions offering continuous education and training in the HCT sector. In some countries, such as Austria, entrepreneurs are required to obtain an entry certificate to the industry from the public authorities. In Switzerland, this practice has been abolished by most local governments. In these countries, and in others with a strong tradition of public training, the social partners run institutions to deliver continuous training, especially at a higher or middle level. Although continuous training features frequently in public debate in Austria, only 5 percent of the workforce had recourse to it in 1996. This may be explained by the reluctance of employers to give workers time for training or to pay for the courses, or it may be caused by the workers' own disinclination to undergo training.

Private and Semi-private Institutions

Private hotel and restaurant training facilities are many and varied and employers as well as students tend to criticize the weakness or absence of public or joint (employer/government) control of private training establishments unless they have the authority to issue government-guaranteed certificates. In Switzerland, tight public control is exercised over the six establishments that issue government certificates. Their owners include government, employers' organizations, a workers' organization, a mixed foundation, and a fully private institution. The remaining private hotel and restaurant schools in Switzerland are not publicly monitored: the Swiss Association of Hotel and Restaurant Schools performs this function. These establishments tend to recruit students from abroad and charge annual fees of up to Sw.frs.20,000. The training provided by the Swiss schools has already assimilated the requirements of the new skills and concentrates on continued general education, languages, and personality skills for managers. On the technical side, the emphasis is on marketing and product development, while more basic skills are dealt with in training blocks.

In the 1960s and 1970s, universities and colleges in the United States were the first to offer hotel and tourism degrees at the tertiary level. Since then, hotel and tourism curricula have been established at college and university level in Germany, Austria and Switzerland. In Spain, tourism schools used to have agreements with British universities to issue college certificates, but they have now linked up with local universities and their work has been integrated into the official Spanish education system. The training at universities, colleges and generally private specialized schools focuses on management of tourism enterprises or developing tourism destinations and also provides a grounding in both conceptual and practical skills geared to a sector dominated by small and medium-sized enterprises. The schools are responding to criticism, heard mainly in developing countries, regarding a lack of practical skills in their graduates. In recently industrialized countries, such as Brazil and China, local centres are upgrading their curricula through cooperation with renowned American and European hotel and restaurant schools.

Tourism education and training provided by trade associations is widely available in many industrialized countries. This in general consists of non-degree programmes of a more practical nature. In the United States, as an outstanding example, the Educational Institute of the American Hotel and Motel Association has provided educational services to almost 300,000 persons within the country and elsewhere. The institute offers its own diplomas and certificates in six areas of specialization using textbooks and distance learning materials produced by leading educators from various universities. Distance training systems with interactive Internet technology and worldwide outreach are starting to operate in all sectors, to the benefit of employees unable to leave work.

New work structures require more direct customer contact. Training institutions will accord greater attention to this area which is critical to improvement in productivity. However, there is little information available about changes in the area of traditional apprenticeships, through which (in Austria, for example) apprentices continue to be trained for the classical occupations of cook or waiter. It is probable, in view of the emphasis on personality and social skills, that training will become less formalized. These changes pose a considerable challenge as regards certification of skills for career purposes.

Training Provided by the Employer

Elaborate human resource development strategies are usually linked to long-term business development plans, and these are more frequently associated with large enterprises. They are based on a budget set aside for training and providing for trainers to be contracted from outside the hotel. Training budgets can account for up to 3 percent of a hotel's financial turnover although 1 percent of payroll is considered substantial. A system of assessing training requirements through frequent staff appraisal is found at establishments where staff development is taken seriously. Where training is less formalized, on the other hand, it is done by managers or supervisors who are not training specialists; there may be no budget set aside for it in spite of a declared willingness to offer training to staff.

In such cases, training is often reactive rather than proactive, i.e. restricted to induction training for newly recruited staff and statutory (compulsory) safety and health training. It is also common for scheduled training sessions to be cancelled when employees are not replaced at their workplaces and therefore fail to turn up. Major hotel chains rely largely on their own internal training systems. The Accor Group employs about 140,000 people in 132 countries. Five percent of staff-related expenditure goes on training in three main areas: initial training for basic qualifications or as an introduction for new employees (delivered in-house); continuous training for director-level employees (department chiefs and others), covering areas such as sales, leadership, customer contacts and so on; and inter-cultural education. Accor's training is delivered by the group's own Paris-based academy which has training centres in various locations and countries. The Accor academy receives 14,000 trainees each year. In addition, the group has concluded agreements with a number of schools to accept Accor personnel for certain courses and to run fellowship programmes for Accor.

An example of the way in which some independent hotels address the problem of skills deficiencies is provided by one group of United Kingdom hotels. The group in question has formed a training consortium which works with a regional college to run an employee training and development programme, thus allowing economies of scale. All the hotels in the group can send one or two staff members to attend the courses as required.

Employers use training as a means of curbing staff turnover and of encouraging staff loyalty to the enterprise so as to maintain a core staff. In some cases, training is also given to casual but frequently employed staff who do not want a permanent contract. Training may also be used as a means to make up for difficult working conditions and low remuneration. However, it should be noted that although most workers have received induction training and safety and health training, specific career-building training was generally provided only for a minority of staff, such as those in the upper hierarchy.

Defining the Training Gap

The hotel and restaurant industry suffers from a discrepancy between training supply and demand. The specialized training institutions tend to lag behind developments in the industry, and these developments are particularly radical at present. The current skills gap is felt to be at the operational level, whereas training institutions, especially private institutions, are largely geared towards management training. This situation is seen in Brazil, where a study shows that training institutions are relevant only for the higher qualification levels and the majority of staff recruited by enterprises have not undergone any formal training.

New Techniques of Training Delivery

Education and training are benefiting from developments in information and communication technologies and are increasingly being delivered through multimedia devices such as interactive on-line connections and CD-ROM. Investments in competitive training packages can be immense: the cost of a recent training CD-ROM for the hotel and restaurant sector was US$1 million. Large chains of hotels are also making use of this technology to fulfil their training needs: Holiday Inn spent US$2.5 million in 1995 to create online training multimedia for its employees. In 1998, Cendant's Days Inn launched an interactive web-based training programme to maximize the efficiency of the training budget and employee time.

Traditional schools are finding themselves in competition with "cyberschools", and where multimedia training devices are used within traditional schools, teachers are moving away from their traditional role as sources of knowledge towards a new role as "coaches" who help students to tap into much better (electronic) sources of knowledge. Hotel and restaurant firms are already developing and using multimedia components to guide employees through everything from making a pizza to providing a help desk for night auditors. Students will be able to chose when and where to undergo their training, and to adapt it to their individual learning speed. Education and training will shift from being teacher-centred to being learner-centred.

In the Netherlands, the Hotel School of The Hague has developed an innovative teaching method. There are no traditional classes. Students are set problems individually or in groups and then seek the information they need to solve them, coached by former teachers. In order to do this they have to develop technical and behavioural skills of various kinds and in different areas which hitherto were taught separately. Students are expected to return to the school throughout their professional life for recycling and "lifelong learning", supported by more or less permanent on-line learning. Increased motivation has been noted both among staff and students. However, performance measurement was harder, and prospective employers will have to adjust their selection criteria in order to assess the new type of training.

Conditions for electronically supported learning are almost ripe for a further "quantum leap". The interconnection of individuals and the formation of virtual learning groups, as well as the ability to call up from a local workstation all the knowledge accumulated by a company or made available through leasing contracts, will change lifelong learning into a continuous updating of personnel. Expert support will be made available on line and in real time, and there will be virtually no limits, other than those of cost, to the instant accessibility of the multimedia training material needed for individual learning plans.

Social Dialogue on Training

Tripartite or bipartite cooperation on training policies is common in many countries, at central or local levels. In many countries, developed or developing, staff training is guided by tripartite bodies, some of them sectoral. In Canada, the Hotel Employees and Restaurant Employees International Union, the Canadian Auto Workers (CAW) and the United Food and Commercial Workers sit beside management on the board of the Canadian Tourism Human Resource Council (CTHRC) which provides labour-oriented input to new certification and training programmes.

The dual system of initial training common in a number of European countries has long been based on a firm consensus between employers' and workers' organizations and on detailed legislation. Proposals for changes in pertinent legislation go through solid consultation procedures before they can be adopted by the competent authorities. Quicker action and intensive consultation is required in the sphere of continuous training, particularly where the improvement of workers' skills is part of a broader strategy for the development of the hotel, catering and tourism sector on a national or regional basis.

Spain provides an example of an effort to rapidly improve the quality of the tourism product in the face of increased international competition. Joint sectoral committees composed of delegates from representative workers' and employers' organizations, technically supported by the Foundation for Continuous Training (FORCEM), appraise training plans with a view to submitting recommendations for public funding to a central (inter-sectoral) joint committee. The sectoral committees propose certification criteria for continuous training courses in accordance with a national qualification system. Women's training heads the list amongst the target group criteria of the Spanish joint committee on hotels and restaurants.

In a number of Latin American countries, tripartite committees on vocational training have been in existence for decades and have influenced some vocational training policies. However, as most efficient vocational training systems were run by sectoral employers' organizations using payroll-based funding modalities (Brazil, Colombia), unions felt that their participation in steering committees did not always have the desired effect. Designing standards for competencies is a new area in which tripartite cooperation is developing at a rather technical level. In the European Union, an important step was taken by the ECF-IUF and the European Federation of Contract Catering Organizations (FERCO). In 1999 they concluded an "Agreement on vocational training in the European contract catering sector," which provides for joint initiatives in the area of continuous vocational training.

In particular, it refers to non-discrimination between men and women, full-time and part-time employees and professional categories, in respect of access to continuous training measures. Before the agreement, the ECF-IUF prepared a survey on continuous training in the European contract catering industry based on a questionnaire. It produced a very heterogeneous picture across the countries in terms of regulations (none at all, legislation or collective agreements), volume (in terms of percentage of payroll spent on continuous training), distribution (between blue-collar and white-collar workers), participation of workers' representatives in planning, certification, and other areas. The survey concluded that continuous training was provided by enterprises, and that the skills required were not recognized officially. It noted that such training still helped workers to advance in their careers or to find alternative employment. However, such training did not fully meet workers' expectations, and there was inadequate trade union involvement.

Social Dialogue

The social dialogue relationship between the social partners in the hotel, catering and tourism sector in general seems to need more development. Both workers and employers agree that much remains to be done. There are differences, however. Trade unions' concerns are centred on being recognized as partners for social dialogue everywhere, as pointed out below. Employers generally favour greater social responsibility of the enterprise, but not all employers actively promote partnership with trade unions as a means of achieving their social goals. Whatever the current and future shape of partnerships, the understanding of the International Hotel and Restaurant Association (IH&RA) is that the social role of enterprises will be determined by a general trend towards democratization.

Employers also see better partnership between management and labour arising from a common response to the challenges of global competition. They anticipate that workers' organizations will adjust to the discipline that capital markets impose on business, while trade unions are worried by practices such as subcontracting and franchising which they feel create divisions among those working at the same location.

They also favour the ratification by ILO member States of the Working Conditions (Hotels and Restaurants) Convention, 1991 (No. 172), and the promotion of equality between women and men at the workplace.

A trend towards improving social partnership can be observed in the Caribbean, where the tourism industry is by far the most important economic sector and where employers' "increasing recognition of the need to engage the cooperation of labour is matched by an increasing recognition on the part of labour that the transformation of business into more productive and competitive operations could mean higher levels of employment and income security".

Organizations

The coverage by workers' and employers' organizations of the hotel, catering and tourism sector can vary from country to country and from region to region. In general, workers' organizations are more diverse than employers' associations. For historical reasons, trade unions either:

(a) cover a number of sectors, of which the hotel, catering and tourism sector is only one; such is the case of those trade unions that represent the entire food production chain from farms to restaurants or groceries; or

(b) cover a proportion of workers in the hotel, catering and tourism sector as a result of overlapping with their main sectors, such as office workers (travel agencies), transport workers, workers in services in general (France) or in personal services in particular (Austria).

On the other hand, employers' organizations in the HCT sector are more uniform, as hotels and restaurants form a clear majority amongst their membership. As far as the restaurant subsector is concerned, however, representation of employers in a number of countries is subdivided into three different types of specialized organizations covering conventional restaurants, collective or institutional catering, and, more recently, fast-food restaurants, as in Germany.

At the European level, there are two federations of employers' organizations: the Confederation of National Associations of Hotels, Restaurants, Cafes and Similar Establishments in the European Union and European Economic Area (HOTREC), for conventional hotels and restaurants; and the European Federation of Contract Catering organizations (FERCO), for collective or institutional restaurants.

The International Hotel and Restaurant Association (IH&RA) is the largest organization of hotel and restaurant employers at the international level, representing over 750,000 establishments in more than 150 countries.

Among its affiliates are some 50 national and international hotel and restaurant chains, many independent hotel operators and restaurateurs, over 110 national hotel and restaurant associations, a number of industry suppliers, and 130 educational institutions in the hotel and restaurant industry.

The largest workers' organization at the international level, the International Union of Food, Agricultural, Hotel, Restaurant, Catering, Tobacco and Allied Workers' Associations (IUF), has 326 affiliated organizations representing 10 million workers in 118 countries.

Other international trade secretariats, the International Transport Workers' Federation (ITF), and Union Network International (UNI), which represents workers in travel agencies, coordinate their action with the IUF. At the European level, this coordination has resulted in a special European Trade Union Liaison Committee on Tourism (ETLC).

Obstacles to Workers' Organizing

Workers in the hospitality sector are in general organized in trade unions to a lesser degree than workers in other sectors. This is due to a number of circumstances including the following:

The small size of enterprises: Owing to the prevalence of small enterprises, trade union affiliation in the HCT sector may be as little as 10 percent on average in industrialized countries. However, major hotels in large cities are often unionized, even in countries where smaller units or hotels located outside the centres of large cities are not.

For example, in Canada (Vancouver, Toronto and Montreal), an estimated 80 percent of large full-service downtown and airport hotels were unionized in the mid-1990s. In the United Kingdom, the role of trade unions is stronger in institutional catering, mainly in the public sector, and in a minority of large hotel groups.

The mainly young workforce: Most workers in the HCT sector lack experience with labour issues as they are in their first formal employment, which in most cases is still of a transient nature.

High staff turnover: Even those workers who stay in the sector will change employers frequently or leave work altogether during certain periods of their life; this is notably the case with women when their children are small.

Prevalence of part-time and casual work, irregular hours: Part-time or on-call arrangements, as well as irregular working hours, keep communication between workers at a low level. In particular, the increasing number of students working in the sector are not necessarily inclined to join trade unions.

Varying employment contracts: Subcontracting, fixed-term employment, and internships in many modern hotel and restaurant enterprises split workers up into several segments with different employment conditions, even when they perform the same tasks. This results in individualization of workers and competition between them.

Gender: Weak affiliation to workers' organizations is more common among women workers since they are disproportionately represented among parttime, casual and young workers and in small enterprises. As they form the less qualified and less well-remunerated segment of the labour force, they also tend to have less access to information and are less able to contribute to workers' collective bargaining power.

Attitude factors: Low self-esteem among the workforce as a collectivity is specific to the hotel and restaurant sector. This is due, firstly, to its generally poor image from which only modern enterprises are immune.

The sector is still associated with service in the traditional sense, which involves a "submissive" relationship . Secondly, success in hotel and restaurant services is hard to measure objectively, as it depends on the subjective feelings of customers. The modern customer relationship is built on individual capacities, skills and style, and there is little collective kudos to be had from excellent service.

These factors are reflected in the attitudes of many employers who do not favour the organization of workers in independent bodies with roots outside the enterprise. This is particularly marked in small and medium-sized enterprises and in multinational enterprises whose central management is not used to a trade union culture. Some observers stress the paternalistic management style prevalent in small hotels and restaurants as a factor working against any collective workers' representation.

Subcontracting and Franchising

Trade unions in the hotel and restaurant sector take the view that subcontracting is a method increasingly used to divide workers and thereby weaken collective bargaining power. Moreover, subcontractor enterprises are normally less unionized or belong to a different sector from that of the contracting enterprise.

As a result, they tend to pay lower wages and provide less stable employment conditions.

Increasingly, subcontracted services relate to security and surveillance, maintenance, cleaning, catering for hotel personnel and restaurant services for guests. As profit margins are considerably lower for restaurants than for hotel operations, subcontracting of restaurants is being increasingly used in large and medium-sized hotels.

The Hotel Employees and Restaurant Employees International Union (HERE) in the United States and Canada acknowledges that leasing out a hotel restaurant is economically attractive where the hotel is unionized and the leasing enterprise is not. The phenomenon is "exacerbated [for the unions] because in most major North American cities the restaurant industry is largely non-union".

At the "New York- New York" Casino in Las Vegas, for example, where virtually all food and beverage services have been subcontracted, HERE represents 900 workers; it would represent 2,700 workers in the hotel if food and beverages were not leased out.

Safeguarding workers' interests in the context of subcontracting has become one of the main objectives of collective bargaining in the hospitality sector. Trade unions are not opposed to subcontracting in principle but want to negotiate the modalities in order to protect workers against dismissal or deterioration of employment and working conditions. The IUF regards subcontracting as a priority area.

Some of HERE's local affiliates bargain to establish joint liability of the employer and the subcontractor. Agreements include a commitment on the part of the (old) employer, e.g. "to require such contractor to offer employment to existing personnel, to recognize their length of service, and to recognize the union as the collective bargaining agent".

The franchising system creates similar difficulties with regard to worker representation as subcontracting, especially where legislation provides for company-wide workers' representative bodies based on minimum numbers of employees per unit. Franchised units have the legal status of independent employers, although in terms of their workplace activities they are an integrated part of a larger company.

Trade unions therefore believe that there is an imbalance between the actual size of a company and the legal status of its smaller units. Franchised units benefit from the support of central management in areas such as labour relations, marketing, technological innovation and standardization of procedures.

However, agreements concluded between trade unions and companies such as Accor or McDonald's apply only to those units that are owned centrally, not to other franchised units which may well represent the majority of all units, as is the case with McDonald's.

The IUF therefore proposes to its affiliates a strategy aimed at creating the same social conditions for workers in franchised units as for the workers in units fully owned by the multinational company in question, in accordance with the principle "same brand-same rights". The example of McDonald's is illustrative. By the end of 1999 the McDonald's Corporation employed well over one and a half million workers in more than 25,000 units in over 110 countries (about half of all of the units were in the United States). Some 70-80 percent of its outlets are franchised, and the company owns 60 percent of the sites.

Workers' Representation at the Enterprise Level

It has been pointed out in previous sections of this report that the hospitality sector, with its subdivision into relatively small units, its service industry character and its flexible orientation towards the customer, has been guided by teamwork for a long time. Bodies that organize workers within the enterprise on the basis of teamwork structures, such as quality circles, are therefore more common than formalized works councils. Workers' representation at the employer's initiative rarely addresses fundamental interests such as pay or working time. It is intended more to improve communication between staff and management and among staff members, and to deal with questions concerning the improvement of day-to-day business operations and staff training.

For example, the British Hospitality Association (representing 25,000 establishments in the United Kingdom) advises that the issues dealt with in consultation with the workers should be selected at the discretion of the employer and as required by legislation.

The actual presence and activity of employees in non-elected workers' participation structures seems to vary considerably depending on the subject dealt with, whether the meeting takes place during working hours, at what time of day, and other factors. Participation is therefore largely on an ad hoc basis. An Accor hotel manager in Paris, referring to meetings with staff on hotel refurbishing options, stated that as a rule one-third of the staff had participated actively, another third remained rather passive but were present at the meetings, and the rest did not attend.

Where staff representation in the enterprise is based on the election of representatives, whether required by law or not, trade unions are generally involved even where their candidates do not stand for election under the trade union label.

The existence of works councils in turn greatly facilitates the activities of workers' organizations, including trade unions, and is a precondition for a high affiliation rate. According to the Nahrung, Genus, Gaststätten (NGG) trade union in Germany, referring to the setting up of a works council at McDonald's, trade union membership becomes well established and increases rapidly after a works council is created, rising on average from almost zero to around 50 percent or more.

However, legislation on works councils is applicable only to enterprises with a minimum number of employees. Given that the hotel, restaurant and tourism sector is dominated by rather small enterprises, most of its workers in reality are not yet participating in social dialogue.

Collective Bargaining

Collective bargaining in the hotel, catering and tourism sector varies according to the social dialogue culture of a country or region. Collective agreements often differ from each other according to local conditions or enterprise cultures. Trade unionists say that the great variety of collective agreements in the sector may reflect a low level of coordination across geographic and enterprise borders and ultimately follows from low trade union density.

Collective agreements are not yet fully applied to ensure decent working conditions for all and competitive human resource development, even where appropriate clauses are contained in the text. They normally cover mainly remuneration and working conditions, as well as nondiscrimination and, more recently, the prohibition of child labour.

Training provided by the employer is mentioned only in a minority of collective agreements. Among the working conditions reflected in most agreements, working time predominates owing to the prevailing irregular working hours and the difficulty of assessing overtime and guaranteeing rest periods. Works councils, where they exist, are often given ad hoc power to agree to changes at short notice.

Remuneration is determined in collective agreements according to occupational group, hierarchical level and personal criteria such as age and seniority. The definition of these criteria often creates difficulties, as classifications of occupations are not generally agreed by the social partners in all countries. Especially in the HCT sector, the definition of occupations is becoming increasingly fluid as phenomena such as multiskilling and flexible distribution of tasks in the enterprise prevail as a result of restructuring and new management methods imposed by competition. Trade unions are concerned with providing, through collective bargaining, minimum definitions in order to prevent salaries from deteriorating as a result of unclear notions of new work patterns. The classifications of occupations reflected in collective agreements are generally established by bipartite or tripartite bodies, often within the framework of vocational training policies.

The structure and scope of collective bargaining in the HCT sector varies according to legislation and national practice. In North America, Asia and Africa, the workforce of an enterprise tends to be the representative group for the purposes of bargaining. In European countries, on the other hand, negotiations are frequently undertaken on behalf of all workers in the sector or of a subsector on a geographical basis, i.e. at national or regional level.

In Germany, collective agreements with geographical coverage at the regional (Lander) level stipulate minimum regulations and are complemented by collective agreements at the enterprise level. Recently, there has been a tendency to negotiate more issues at the enterprise level than was done in the past in order to take account of sharper differences between the economic performance of individual enterprises.

Collective bargaining in the HCT sector is based on the subsectors covered by employers' organizations, so that separate negotiations are often held for hotels and restaurants, catering and the tour operating and travel agency subsector. Chain enterprises may engage in collective bargaining, leaving small and medium-sized enterprises behind; this has been the case in France, where collective agreements were concluded for a number of years for hotel and restaurant chains, while the independent hotels and restaurants adopted the procedure only recently.

As many as 80 percent of independent (predominantly small) enterprises are covered by the collective agreements, although their workers are normally not unionized. In addition, the collective agreement is regularly extended by Government decree to cover all enterprises and all workers in the sector.

Collective bargaining and collective agreements have been useful in mitigating the negative effects on workers of increased competition between enterprises resulting from globalization, and in preventing an unbalanced distribution between employers and workers of the burden resulting from rapid changes. A common challenge arises when ownership of an enterprise changes. In such cases, a general clause is sometimes introduced in collective agreements to guarantee the preservation of employment contracts and other arrangements for a certain period.

One example of this is an agreement between the Italian-based company, Autogrill and the Dutch trade union federation, Horecabond in 1998. Following Autogrill's purchase of the Dutch company AC Holding, the agreement guaranteed that no worker would be dismissed within a period of two-and-a-half years and that existing employment conditions and workers' rights would remain in force during that period. Collective agreements addressing similar situations have been concluded in other European countries.

Trade unions have had difficulties in bargaining on the continuity of working and employment conditions in cases where they are faced with a weak local interlocutor and the acting party behind the change is a multinational enterprise based outside the country. This situation may arise in cases of franchising or in cases of management contracts with strict decentralization of power with regard to labour relations.

It is generally the policy of transnational companies to leave labour relations to the local level to ensure that local conditions are taken fully into account.

Trade unions object to this policy, however, where it puts workers in a subsidiary of a multinational enterprise in a less favourable position than other workers of the same chain, or where the mother enterprise's absence from labour relations leaves the local employer in a weak position or unwilling to assume contractual responsibility.

Social dialogue in the hotel, catering and tourism sector does not provide for collective bargaining at the international level at present, apart from agreements concerning the recognition of trade unions and the right of employees to exercise trade union mandates.

Social Dialogue Plus: Community Involvement

Organizations involved in campaigning for changes in the hotel, catering and tourism sector can find partners and supporters in different segments of the community because the sector overlaps with many others. This is more likely in countries where tourism is the most dynamic sector or where it is the major source of foreign exchange income, as is the case in many small island States, such as those of the Caribbean. An interesting example is the "living wage campaign" conducted in the 1990s in the hospitality sector in Los Angeles.

Regional Social Dialogue: The Case of Europe

At the level of the European Union and the European Economic Area (EEA), employers and workers of the hotel, restaurants and cafes sector engage in social dialogue at the sectoral level within a framework provided by the European Commission. A formal social dialogue committee at sectoral level was set up in 1999 after social dialogue activities had been launched by the social partners (ECFIUF and HOTREC) in the early 1990s.

The group meets four times a year for sessions conducted by the European Commission. The results of sectoral social dialogue at European level include various joint declarations adopted by the social partners since 1995. The most recent one, dated 3 May 1999, is the Joint Declaration for the promotion of employment in the European hotel and restaurant sector.

It reflects the major social issues concerning this sector at present. In order to achieve improved competitiveness and efficiency of European enterprises, provide better qualified and motivated staff and create new job opportunities, the social partners propose to adopt certain measures concerning, in particular, the reduction of taxes and non-wage costs, and improved training and certification to enhance workers' employability and mobility. Issues of part-time employment and flexible working hours are also addressed.

The creation of full-time jobs remains a priority; the intention is that flexible working hours should be applied within the framework of agreements between the social partners and adapted to the respective needs of companies and employees. An Agreement on vocational training in the European contract catering sector was reached by FERCO and ECF-IUF in October 1999.

The Agreement covers joint initiatives in the area of continuous vocational training, commitments to equal treatment for men and women and for full-time and part-time workers, and commitments to non-discrimination against workers involved in training. It also stimulates joint action at the company level to identify training needs, elaborate programmes and evaluate their effectiveness. Employers' and workers' representatives also participated, through individually named experts or the European Trade Union Liaison Committee on Tourism (ETLC), in the High Level Group on Tourism and Employment convened by the European Commission in 1998.

The resulting recommendations have reportedly been useful in many bipartite or tripartite debates on the development of tourism as an employment-creating activity. They cover issues such as: negotiation of flexible employability systems and a dynamic approach to social protection; promotion of vocational training for career development; mutual recognition of qualifications between European countries to enhance workers' mobility; and structured, sectoral social dialogue.

European Works Councils

Social dialogue within multinational companies at European level is provided for by the EU Directive (94/45, of 1994) on European Works Councils (EWCs), which has initiated cross-border meetings between workers' representatives and managers of companies having business in more than one country within the European Economic Area (including the United Kingdom since the 1997 Amsterdam Treaty).

The essential requirement of the Directive is the creation of a European Works Council in every active enterprise with at least 150 employees in each of at least two countries and a total of at least 1,000 employees within the EEA. A procedure for consultation and information sharing must be established if at least 150 employees from at least two countries request it.

Those meetings are not so much collective bargaining sessions as information and consultation procedures, and employee representatives cannot block management decisions. Most of the

European Works Councils in the hotel, catering and tourism sector were created by multinational companies that established "voluntary agreements" for a transitional period before full implementation of the Directive in September 1996.

Those agreements could be concluded with appointed employee representatives instead of those determined in accordance with national law or practice, as required by the Directive.

At present, there are 14 EWCs of which only two were established after the deadline for voluntary agreements (by Sodexho, the world's largest institutional caterer, and in American Express). The achievements of the EWCs so far have only partially lived up to the expectations of the trade unions involved. This seems to be mainly due to the infrequency of (annual) meetings.

The major concern of trade unions with regard to transnational companies is the loss of jobs in the restructuring process which often follows mergers or acquisitions. Consultation at that juncture is considered by trade unions to be the "litmus test" of how seriously management takes its obligation to consult workers under the terms of the EU Directive.

Positive examples cited by trade union sources include: Club Mediterranean, whose management has consulted and came to an agreement with its EWC on closing operations and restructuring processes; Accor, which has concluded an agreement with IUF on trade union rights based largely on ILO Conventions Nos. 87, 98 and 135; and the policies adopted by the Compass Group.

Internationalization of Information on Labour Issues

Communication technology makes it possible to post information for an international audience without delay. Labour disputes in hotels or restaurants are increasingly drawn to the attention of the public through trade unions websites.

Those sites also contain recommendations on hotels to avoid and those that should be patronized in the light of management attitudes to trade union activities and workers' interests. Detailed accounts of labour disputes are given in cases of non-recommendation by the IUF. Employers' associations object to the practice, which they maintain does not adequately distinguish between labour relations disputes which do not necessarily involve any illegal actions and acts which are "illegal and socially reprehensible".

In response to the limited success of collective bargaining, trade unions have also resorted to international solidarity campaigns. A major labour dispute in the Lotte Hotel in Seoul came to an end on 21 August 2000 after several trade unions posted information on the dispute and the workers' claims on their website and representations were made by trade unions in different countries to Korean diplomatic missions. The agreement provides for an automatic mechanism to stabilize precarious employment of staff.

Information and communication technologies also increase the potential for pressure on tourism destinations that fail to comply with minimum standards. An example of this is the tourism boycott against the military regime in Myanmar pursued by the IUF through the Internet. A number of companies involved in tourism activities in that country and engaged in social dialogue with trade unions affiliated to the IUF have responded by discontinuing their engagement until the social and political situation in the country is stabilized and pending civil rights issues are resolved.

Social Dialogue on Tourism Development Policies

Workers' and employers' organizations are involved in tourism development policies in many countries where tourism boards include workers' and employers' representatives. In a number of cases, the structure was established following ILO technical cooperation. At the international level, workers' and employers' organizations are represented at the annual meetings organized by the United Nations Commission for Sustainable Development (CSD) as a follow-up to the 1992 United Nations Conference on Environment and Development (UNCED), which identified tourism as one of the key economic sectors which could make a positive contribution to achieving sustainable development. At the Seventh Session of the Commission for Sustainable Development (CSD-7, 1999), which dealt with sustainable tourism development among other topics, business and industry was represented by the International Hotel and Restaurant Association (IH&RA) and the World Travel and Tourism Council (WTTC).

Workers were represented by the International Confederation of Free Trade Unions (ICFTU) and the Trade Union Advisory Committee to the OECD (TUAC). During the discussions, the social dimension of sustainable tourism development was widely recognized. Both groups called for training of hotel and tourism personnel in environmental protection, and emphasized the importance of making tourism sustainable so as to maximize its potential for job creation. The workers and trade union representatives noted a deterioration of working conditions and labour rights in tourism arising from globalization and from competition among countries for foreign investment. The business group presented its environmental initiatives – WTTC's "Green Globe" label and the annual environmental award "Green Hotelier" given by IH&RA and UNEP – and set out its views on the criteria for sustainable growth in the industry and many voluntary initiatives undertaken by it.

4

Tourism in Developing Countries

Although the hotel, catering and tourism (HCT) sectors produce an estimated 3-4 of GDP in most of the world economy and employ approximately 3 percent of the world's total labour force, its workers earn "on average at least 20 percent less than workers in other economic sectors," .

And while technology, deregulation and globalization are fuelling growth prospects in some up-market segments of the tourist trade, the prospects for smaller and medium-sized enterprises (which produce most of the employment benefits) are increasingly unclear.

The wage differential is due to the "higher proportion of unskilled workers" employed in the HCT sector, where working conditions are often characterized by part-time or low-paid jobs. "Up to half the workers in the industry are under 25 years old and up to 70 percent are women,".

Migrant workers are another vulnerable group which tends to be overly-proportionately employed in the sector, with migrants concentrated in lower paid and less stable segments of the job market due to such factors as language or unfamiliarity with the host culture.

Often very young children work in the tourism sector, particularly in small, family-based enterprises, but often on their own as vendors or helpers: "The worst form of child labour in tourism is seen in the sex trade," the report notes. Though the problem is widespread, the report notes the increasing indignation of the international community at this exploitation and highlights "the increasing participation of international employers and workers' organizations and the World Tourism Organization in combatting child prostitution in tourism".

Other labour problems affecting the industry are high staff turnover, irregular working hours, low levels of unionization (less than 10 percent) and intense pressure on human and environmental resources as tourism becomes increasingly competitive and reaches into far flung destinations where institutional resources are weak or inadequate.

The true scope of the economic and employment importance of tourism becomes even larger when one considers that each job in the sector, generates an estimated one-and-a-half additional (indirect) jobs in tourism related sectors and in some regions tourism provides direct employment to as much as 10 percent of the workforce.

If both direct and indirect employment is taken into account, "the total tourism related economy has been estimated to produce as much as 11 percent of GDP and to employ 8 percent of the labour force worldwide," according to the World Travel and Tourism Council.

In recent years, the highest annual growth rates have been registered in South Asia (9 percent), the Caribbean (7 percent) and Eastern Europe (5 percent). In contrast, Europe is growing at around 2 percent and Asia Pacific by only 1.4 percent in the aftermath of the Asian financial crisis.

Cross-border tourism has grown faster than tourism overall, and is expected to increase by 4.5 percent over the next 20 years. "During the year 2000," the report notes, "almost 700 million tourists crossed a border and spent over US$500 billion while abroad". The deregulation of air transport and resulting fall in air fares is a major contributing factor to the globalization of tourism: "In developing countries no less than 80 percent of international tourists arrive by air."

The quality of tourism services is also changing rapidly, with travel becoming a regular part of the lifestyle of populations in wealthier nations and the better-off in developing countries, the ILO report finds.

Trips are becoming shorter but more frequent, with new market niches, such as nature tourism, ecotourism and adventure tourism flourishing in response to consumer demand and often yielding substantial benefits to populations in remote rural areas where agricultural incomes tend to be declining. According to the ILO report "the spread of information technologies enables tourism providers to cater more efficiently for a more diversified clientele". However, these benefits are not evenly spread.

The report cites concerns about "the relatively low participation of developing countries in electronic distribution and reservation systems run by large air carriers, which do not sufficiently take into account the needs of small and medium-sized enterprises (SMEs)".

While large hotel chains are constantly increasing the scope and efficiency of their operations through mergers, franchising arrangements and increased linkages between air carriers, hotels, travel agencies and retail distributors, "independent enterprises tend to be left behind,". This is troublesome because it is precisely the SMEs that "employ at least half the sector's workforce and represent a majority of its enterprises".

Tourism in the Developing World

Although often underestimated, the tourism industry can help promote

- peace and stability in developing countries by providing jobs, generating income, diversifying the economy, protecting the environment, and promoting cross-cultural awareness. Tourism is the fourthlargest industry in the global economy.
- However, key challenges must be addressed if peace-enhancing benefits from this industry are to be realized. These include investments in infrastructure and human capacity, the development of comprehensive national strategies, the adoption of robust regulatory frameworks,

mechanisms to maximize in-country foreign currency earnings, and efforts to reduce crime and corruption.

- The case studies of India, Kenya, and Nigeria reveal several important points. First, relative peace and a degree of economic development are preconditions for a successful tourist industry. Second, although it has the capacity to help promote peace and prosperity, tourism can also cause a great deal of harm unless it is carefully developed. Third, to deliver optimal benefits, tourism must be respectful of the environment and mindful of cultural and social traditions. Fourth, tourism must be supported by a coherent national strategy and robust laws.
- For tourism to help deliver prosperity and stabilize communities effectively, specific action must be taken by three main constituencies: host communities, host governments, and foreign stakeholders. Host communities should work to leverage their competitive advantage, improve service delivery, and protect their environment and culture. Host governments should establish supportive strategies, introduce and implement necessary regulations, remove bottlenecks, and adopt internationally recognized tourism standards. Foreign stakeholders could prioritize tourism as a viable economic force, direct investment to this sector, and facilitate knowledge and technological transfers.

Tourism is a vital part of the global economy. Generating roughly $1 trillion in global receipts in 2008 (up 1.8 percent from 2007), international tourism ranked as the fourth-largest industry in the world, after fuels, chemicals, and automotive products.

1. The breadth of international travel also has greatly expanded in recent years to encompass the developing world. In 1950 just fifteen destinations—primarily European—accounted for 98 percent of all international arrivals. By 2007 that figure had fallen to 57 percent.
2. Once essentially excluded from the tourism industry, the developing world has now become its major growth area.

> Tourism is a key foreign exchange earner for 83 percent of developing countries and the leading export earner for one-third of the world's poorest countries. For the world's forty poorest countries, tourism is the second-most important source of foreign exchange after oil.

The economic might of the tourist industry has helped transform societies, often for the better. Tourism has several advantages over other industries: It is consumed at the point of production so that it directly benefits the

- communities that provide the goods.
- It enables communities that are poor in material wealth but rich in culture, history, and heritage to use their unique characteristics as an income-generating comparative advantage.
- It creates networks of different operations, from hotels and restaurants to adventure sports providers and food suppliers. This enables tourist centres to form complex and varied supply chains of goods and services, supporting a versatile labour market with a variety of jobs for tour guides, translators, cooks, cleaners, drivers, hotel managers, and other service sector workers. Many tourism jobs are flexible or seasonal and can be taken on in parallel with existing occupations, such as farming.
- It tends to encourage the development of multiple-use infrastructure that benefits the host community, including roads, health care facilities, and sports centres, in addition to the hotels and high-end restaurants that cater to foreign visitors.

With these benefits in mind, the United Nations has identified the development of tourism as one of the methods poorer countries might use to meet the Millennium Development Goals (MDGs). For the first MDG—alleviating poverty—the merits of tourism are evident. It can provide jobs and generate income for communities that, in some cases, lack viable alternative means of employment. In an assessment of Nigeria's potential for tourism, Francesco Frangialli, the former head of the UN World Tourism Organization, argued that with its "capacity to spread its socioeconomic benefits to all levels of society ... tourism can be a leading industry in the fight against poverty." With its tendency to produce flexible labour markets and offer diverse working opportunities, tourism can also help realize a second MDG, that of promoting gender equality.

In Mali, the World Tourism Organization's Sustainable Tourism for Eliminating Poverty (ST-EP) program has supported an effort to train the female artisans of Djenne, one of Mali's oldest and most visited towns. In Costa Rica, women's handicraft cooperatives catering to the tourist market have flourished, providing many women, for the first time, with both independent incomes and improved self-esteem.

If carefully managed, tourism can also be an important part of promoting a sustainable environment, another of the MDGs. Frangialli identified tourism's potential for not only protecting the natural environment, but also "preserving historical, archaeological, and religious monuments; and stimulating the practice of local folklore, traditions, arts and crafts, and cuisine."

Finally, as tourism by definition involves the transfer of people, culture, and ideas, it is ideally placed to foster effective global partnerships, the eighth MDG. In addition to advancing development goals, some have credited tourism with helping to build and sustain peace.

Among them is Wangari Maathai, the Nobel laureate and founder of the Green Belt Movement, who highlights tourism's potential as "a great vehicle for peace promotion." Whether tourism can actually bring about peace or whether the relationship is better described as mutually reinforcing, Corazon Gatchalian and Cindi Reiman conclude that through its tendency to promote "communication between nations and cultures," tourism is an instrument that "creates a global language of peace."

That said, while tourism can bring positive benefits, good does not necessarily follow. In recent years, tourism has tended to be a delivery mechanism for some of the darker effects of globalization: health pandemics and terrorism. International travelers enabled the outbreaks of severe acute respiratory syndrome (SARS) and swine flu to spread rapidly across borders. And holiday destinations, tragically, have become a popular target for terrorists, who want to maximize civilian casualties and publicity for their actions. In recent years, Mumbai, Bali, Sharm el-Sheikh, Dahab, Mombasa, and Casablanca have come to be associated as much with mass bombings and killings as with tourism.

Ecotourism

While conventional mass tourism often negatively affects host environments, other forms of tourism have emerged in recent decades that are more sensitive to their surroundings and offer tangible benefits to the local labour force.

These newer forms of tourism have come to be known as ecotourism, an umbrella term best defined as responsible travel to natural areas that conserves the environment and improves the well-being of local people.

Since it first emerged in the late 1970s, ecotourism has spawned several other travel concepts that are, in essence, variations on the same theme. These include geotourism, pro-poor tourism, sustainable tourism, responsible tourism, and travelers' philanthropy.

They are united by the simple idea that tourism should offer a benefit—and not incur a cost—to the host community. They reflect the desire of many holiday goers to give something back to the places they visit, or at the very least, avoid doing them harm. A number of countries have tailored their tourism industries adeptly to reflect this desire and have reaped economic rewards while minimizing the environmental and social impacts of growth. Costa Rica led the way in developing the ecotourism concept, followed closely by Ecuador, Tanzania, Kenya, and Nepal.

Kenya, Nigeria, and India are three developing countries with tourism industries at different stages of maturity. Kenya has a long-established and highly successful tourist sector catering to the conventional and ecotourism markets. As the table demonstrates, international tourism is a lucrative source of income for Kenya, accounting for 2.24 percent of the nation's gross domestic product (GDP) in 2006. By contrast, Nigeria barely has a tourist industry at all, reflected by tourism's paltry contribution to national wealth, just .02 percent of GDP in 2006. India has several tourist centres but, given its vast size, it has yet to realize tourism's economic potential. International receipts from tourism made up just 0.35 percent of its GDP in 2006.

In Kenya, which has had a longer time to finesse its strategy, ecotourism is starting to bring about the progress that Honey describes. Conservationist David Western, the author of a study of Kenya's tourism industry, explains how Kenya learned from some of the mistakes it made when it began building its safari-based tourism industry.

He discusses how Kenya became the first country in Africa to establish both an ecotourism society and a framework for assessing the social and environmental impact of resort developments. He also illustrates the importance of generating domestic tourism by offering free or heavily discounted national park fees to its citizens.

Most important, he shows how Kenyan communities have benefited directly from tourism by running their own wildlife conservation areas. However, the picture he paints is not overwhelmingly rosy. While pockets of good practice exist, a fair share of Kenya's tourism tramples on local customs, is indifferent to conservation, and fails to pass on economic benefits to host communities.

Planning in Tourism

Planning is the dynamic process of determining goals, systematically selecting alternative courses of actions to achieve those goals, implementing the chosen alternatives and evaluating the choice to determine if it if successful. The planning process regards the environment which includes political, physical, social and economic elements as interrelated and interdependent components which should be taken into account in considering the future of a destination area.

Reasons for Tourism Planning

Tourism planning is greatly needed. The stagnation and decline of a destination or attraction may be due to the lack of planning or poor planning.

Good Practice Guide On Planning for Tourism

Tourism, in all its forms, is of crucial importance to the economic, social and environmental well-being of the whole country. The planning system has a vital role to play in terms of facilitating the development and improvement of tourism in appropriate locations. This chapter is designed to:

- ensure that planners understand the importance of tourism and take this fully into account when preparing development plans and taking planning decisions;
- ensure that those involved in the tourism industry understand the principles of national planning policy as they apply to tourism and how these can be applied when preparing individual planning applications;
- ensure that planners and the tourism industry work together effectively to facilitate, promote and deliver new tourism developments in a sustainable way.

The Local Value of Tourism

Tourism can bring many broader benefits that will contribute to the economic and social well being of local communities as well as to individuals. It can:

- be the focus of regeneration of urban and rural areas, as has been demonstrated by its success in Birmingham and in many seaside resorts;
- provide a catalyst for growth in an area, raising its profile and stabilising out-migration;
- provide opportunities for retraining for the resident workforce and help to diversify over-specialised economies; and
- help maintain and expand underused sports and recreation facilities in urban areas; and

The revenue generated by tourism can help to:

- support and enhance local services and facilities such as shops and pubs, particularly in rural areas;
- secure the retention or upgrading of public services such as public transport, health centres and libraries;
- support a broader and more vibrant and active community by attracting arts, sports or cultural events;
- aid diversification within the rural economy; and
- underpin the quality of the local environment and facilitate further enjoyment of it by residents and visitors.

These benefits can be particularly valuable in rural areas as they may provide amenities that people would otherwise not have access to. Tourism depends heavily on the natural and built environment and can also be the key to maintaining and enhancing the environment:

- The economic benefits of tourism in particular can help to sustain and improve both the natural and built physical environment.
- Derelict land and buildings may be brought back into use and the countryside can be better maintained.
- Visitors to historic buildings, archaeology and landscapes can provide income or voluntary effort which help maintain and conserve such assets.
- In rural areas the health of the environment and of the community depends on the viability of the local economy. So areas which attract visitors for their scenic beauty and which enjoy income from tourism will be better able to afford to sustain the local environment.
- Proposals involving high quality design improve the visual and environmental experience for visitors and the local community alike.

Planning for Tourism

The planning system, by taking a pro-active role in facilitating and promoting the implementation of good quality development, is crucial to ensuring that the tourism industry can develop and thrive, thereby maximising these valuable economic, social and environmental benefits. At the same time, the planning system aims to ensure that these benefits are achieved in the most sustainable manner possible.

The example below gives an overview of how one local authority, the London Borough of Greenwich, has worked actively through the planning system to underpin the development of tourism in its area.

Good Practice Guide on Planning for Tourism

The work of the Planning Department has been crucial to its success. This work has included:

- dedicating specific parts of the development plan to tourism and its promotion. This followed from consultation with the tourism sector including the World Heritage Site Steering Group;
- consultation with stakeholders on planning applications and involvement with partners in the preparation of planning briefs;
- preparing a hotel strategy that actively promoted sites to hotel operators & developers. This has led to two new hotels being built and increased visitor spend in the local economy;
- lobbying with private sector partners for improvements in public transport. This has helped secure investment in light rail, underground and river transport services;
- active engagement with small hoteliers and owners of bed and breakfast establishments to give advice on planning matters;
- securing contributions to tourism initiatives throughs 106 agreements, and voluntary contributions for marketing; and
- working with developers and operators to secure local employment and business opportunities

A Planning Framework for Tourism

Principles of the Planning System

Tourism is an important industry. Its future development will be secured by tourism developers engaging with the planning process and by those operating the planning system recognising that importance. This section sets out the principles of the English planning system which governs all forms of development including planning for tourism.

Sustainable development is the core principle underpinning planning. At the heart of sustainable development is the simple idea of ensuring a better quality of life for everyone, now and for future generations. The planning process provides the opportunity to help to make new development more sustainable, both through the preparation of development plans and when decisions are taken on specific schemes. The outcomes should be developments which:

- provide well-designed, safe and accessible development, and create new opportunities that will improve the well being of individuals and the regeneration of communities;
- result in the more efficient use of land and bring forward sufficient land to meet a wide range of expected needs;
- provide a supportive framework for economic growth and successful business;
- create vibrant, vital and viable town centres;
- reduce the need to travel; and
- protect and enhance the natural and built environment and safeguard natural resources.

Plan-led System

The planning system in England aims to realise these objectives of sustainable development through a 'plan-led' system of development plans prepared by regional planning bodies and local planning authorities. These plans lead the subsequent development by setting a framework which helps to provide both an overall strategy for that development and policies for the determination of individual development proposals. Where these plans contain relevant policies, applications for planning permission should be determined in line with the plan unless material considerations indicate otherwise.

These plans have a number of key characteristics:

- they provide developers, businesses and communities with certainty and predictability about future development in an area;
- they are transparent so that users can readily understand them and the information and assumptions upon which they are based;
- they are flexible so that they can be adjusted to meet changing circumstances and priorities. Planning authorities must ensure that plans are kept up to date and report annually on how their plan's policies are being achieved; and
- they are drawn up with community involvement and present a shared vision and strategy of how the area should develop to achieve more sustainable patterns of development.

Development plans should reflect and build upon the Government's statements of national planning policies.

The development plans prepared by regional planning bodies and local planning authorities are known respectively as regional spatial strategies (RSS) and local development frameworks (LDFs). Planning policy statement (PPS) provides advice on the preparation of RSS and planning policy statement (PPS) provides advice on the preparation of LDFs.

The preparation of RSS is a statutory requirement. They:

- provide a broad development strategy for the region for a fifteen to twenty year period;
- should contribute to the achievement of sustainable development;
- are locationally, but not site, specific;

- are focused on delivery mechanisms which make clear what is to be done by whom and when;
- should be well integrated with other regional strategies, including any regional tourism strategy;
- should address sub-regional issues where appropriate; and
- provide a spatial framework to inform the preparation of LDF documents, local transport plans and regional and sub-regional strategies and programmes that have a bearing on land use activities.

Local development frameworks should be:

- based on a clear understanding of the economic, social and environmental needs of the area;
- clear, succinct and easily understood by all;
- underpinned by a comprehensive and credible evidence base; and
- 'front-loaded', seeking consensus on issues and taking key decisions early in the process.

Development plans are expected to take a spatial planning approach which integrates land use policies with other policies and programmes. The aim should be to coordinate spatial plans with urban and rural regeneration strategies, regional economic and housing strategies, community strategies and local transport plans. Wherever possible, spatial plans should be consistent with these other strategies (including any strategies for or relating to tourism) and be drawn up in collaboration with those responsible for them.

Development plans should have a clear vision about the pattern of development they are seeking to achieve in the area and clear objectives for achieving it. These should reflect the needs and problems of the communities in that area.

They should be concerned not just with what can be built where and in what circumstances but also how the range of social, economic and environmental objectives will be achieved through plan policies. The plans should focus on outcomes, with specified indicators so that the progress made by the policies in meeting these desired outcomes can be measured.

Developing Tourism through Strategies and Plans

Regional Spatial Strategies (RSS)

At the regional level, regional planning bodies will need to decide how to deal with tourism in their RSS. Specifically they will have to decide whether:

- to treat tourism as an issue in itself;
- to subsume it within another issue such as economic development; or
- to deal with it as a consideration affecting a number of issues like the economy, the environment, regeneration and transport.

They should do this on the basis of the overall approach that they are taking in their RSS and in the light of the information they have gathered.

Whatever the chosen approach, the RSS should make clear:

- its vision and strategy for tourism in the region;
- how this contributes to broader regional objectives;
- what level of growth in tourism it is trying to achieve; and
- what the spatial characteristics of this will be.

Where the Regional Development Agencies (RDAs) have Produced Regional

Tourism or Visitor Economy Strategies, the RSS should draw on these as well as providing a context when such strategies are reviewed. They provide greater detail than the Regional Economic Strategies and may have specific spatial or locational dimensions. The West Midlands Visitor Economy Strategy contains the following vision for the future of tourism in the region, and an important context for RSS review.

The RSS should also make clear what the key tourism characteristics are and how these are expected to change during the period of the strategy. This should cover:

- what the scale and distribution of tourist activity within the area is and what it is likely to be. The strategy needs to be clear what degree of change it is seeking to oversee, what the nature of that change will be and where it will occur;
- likely future trends and change in volume, distribution and type of activity.

There needs to be an understanding of what the underlying trends are and how the strategy intends to respond to the opportunities which they present;

- what the implications of those trends are for land-use, traffic flows, and the transport system. It should explain the extent to which these trends are (i) dependent upon improvements to the transport network and (ii) where they are likely to increase the need for such improvements;
- identification of areas within the region where there are, or are likely to be, any problems associated with growth or decline in tourism. For example, it might be necessary to reconcile demand for tourist accommodation with the need for affordable housing within an area;
- how increased demand for tourism might be best accommodated. It might be that the provision of accommodation and attractions should be increased in towns adjoining existing resorts in order to spread the benefits and to diffuse pressures;
- environmental impacts of tourism and, where these have adverse effects, how they can be tackled;
- the need to protect key tourism assets. In addition to features that already have statutory protection (e.g. national parks), there will be other features such as the wider environment, the quality of beaches, choice of accommodation, availability of sports and leisure facilities and the presence of 'night life' that are important in sustaining the attractiveness of the area; and
- ways in which tourism can contribute positively to other objectives e.g. economic development, regeneration, rural

diversification, conservation, and environmental improvements.

Local Development Frameworks (LDFS)

LDFs should comprise a number of development plan documents including the core strategy, site specific allocations of land and area action plans. Any need for further development plan documents, or supplementary planning documents, should be identified in the local development scheme, the purpose of which is to inform the public of the planning authority's programme for the production of local development documents.

In a similar way to regional planning bodies, those preparing LDFs will need to decide how to deal with tourism issues within the framework. Like RSS, the approach should seek to produce a plan which is integrated with other strategies that have been prepared for the area, including any that relate to the future of tourism.

In those locations where the future development of tourism is a key issue for the local authority, it will be appropriate for the core strategy to cover tourism issues together with any objectives relevant to tourism. In other local authorities it may be that the plan's broad approach to economic growth and regeneration sets the framework for the future development of tourism. In these cases this relationship should be acknowledged and taken into account in the development of the core strategy.

Those preparing LDFs should consider whether any policies for tourism are needed beyond what is set out in the core strategy. In determining the scope of the work required and what planning documents should be prepared, it will again be necessary first to decide whether tourism is to be addressed as a single issue or as part of a wider topic, such as economic growth. Where site allocations for tourism are made, these should follow from the objectives set out in the core strategy.

In some areas in which tourism and its growth are a key part of the spatial strategy, it may be appropriate to depict this in spatial terms in the core strategy such as in a key diagram. In specific locations where development for tourism is particularly crucial to meeting the plan's objectives, the core strategy could propose an area action plan to focus and programme the elements of that development.

In order to keep policies to a manageable number, authorities should aim to support the policies affecting tourism in the core strategy in the following ways:

- putting detail on matters such as mitigating the effects of development (e.g. by landscaping) into supplementary planning documents;
- putting good practice messages in other documents or in supporting text; and
- not repeating national or regional policies in LDFs, although LDFs should indicate how the objectives and any targets for tourism contribute to those set out in the RSS.

Where tourism is an important element of a LDF, the approach will need to be based upon a robust understanding of the characteristics of, and trends within, the tourism industry based on similar issues to those set out in RSS.

Bournemouth offers an example of where such an analysis of trends has occurred. This has provided the basis for the planned approach of diversifying tourism facilities at an important tourism destination whilst at the same time retaining the essential tourist accommodation. Although this was done through its preparation of its Local Plan and Supplementary Planning Guidance under the previous system of development plans, the approach in terms of analysis and response would be equally applicable to a LDF approach.

Devising Good Tourism Policies

General Principles

The strategy for tourism in the emerging development plan will provide the context for producing any specific policies for tourism. Whilst policies need to be developed to suit the particular circumstances of an area, there will be certain common features of a good tourism policy. Where specific tourism policies are included in a plan, they should aim to:

- maximise the benefits of tourism, in particular ensuring that the development is able to reach its potential to contribute to tourism in the area and for local communities to enjoy those benefits;
- identify optimal locations, for example to maximise synergies with other tourist attractions and to promote opportunities for access by public transport;
- integrate development with its surroundings both in terms of design and layout and in the way that the service or facility is able to function; and
- avoid adverse impacts, for example by disturbance to activities on adjacent land.

Planners will need to understand and often reconcile a number of important factors when preparing such policies, in particular:

- market demand – sometimes market demand will exist in a very precise location. This might be to do with prominence or accessibility. In other cases the demand will be of approximately the same level throughout a wide area;
- environmental impact – this can have a large number of facets, such as visual and noise impact, impacts on an historic setting, impact upon biodiversity and upon landscape quality. Impacts may be positive, negative or a mix of both;
- transport and accessibility – travel is an inherent element of tourism.

Whilst recognising that it is a principle of the planning system to seek to promote more sustainable transport choices, improve accessibility and reduce the need to travel, this may be particularly difficult for some types of tourism projects or for areas that are poorly served by public transport;

- functional links – whilst some forms of tourism may, in commercial terms, be able to be directed to a variety of locations (e.g. a hotel) others will be much more specific in their land use requirements (e.g. a visitor centre for a cathedral);

- regeneration benefits – tourism developments have the potential to bring jobs to an area, to improve physical appearance and to support local businesses and services. Plans to bring tourism into an area will often be developed in order to realise some of these advantages; and
- labour supply – the amount and quality of the labour supply will vary from place to place. Planning will often seek to locate new development where the need for jobs exist or where the population might benefit from a wider range and quality of employment.

The importance of these factors may vary for different developments and over time.

Tourists visit different areas for different reasons and to enjoy different experiences. It follows that the built infrastructure required for tourism will therefore vary from area to area. Tourism is certainly not a 'one-size fits all' product. In particular, different approaches may be needed in urban areas from those in rural areas.

Tourism in Urban Areas

Tourism can bring benefits to urban areas and help to deliver development that is sustainable. Amongst the particular advantages that tourism can bring to towns and cities is to:

- be the focus of regeneration, or help to underpin it;
- help to increase urban vitality and support linked trips;
- be a key ingredient of mixed-use schemes;
- support important services and facilities; and
- facilitate improved access by sustainable modes of transport.

There are many types of tourist and leisure activities that particularly lend themselves to urban locations and which exhibit these advantages. These include:

- hotel, guest house and bed & breakfast accommodation;
- cinemas, theatres and concert and bingo clubs;
- museums, galleries and conference facilities;
- restaurants, bars, pubs, casinos and night clubs; and
- indoor and ten-pin bowling and health & fitness centres.

Planning authorities need to ensure that they have assessed the need for these facilities and have allocated an appropriate range of sites which allow genuine choices to meet those needs.

Similarly, it is for developers and operators to ensure that they have anticipated what their need for such sites is likely to be and that they undertake active discussions with local planning authorities about these requirements.

Tourism in Rural Areas

The provision of essential facilities for visitors is vital for the development of the tourism in rural areas. Tourism can:

- be a key element in rural and farm diversification;
- help to revitalize market towns and villages;
  - support important rural services and facilities; and
  - underwrite environmental schemes and improvements to the built and natural environment. RSS and LDF policies should therefore engender a positive approach to rural tourism proposals, applying the following principles:
- Wherever possible, tourist and visitor facilities should be housed in existing or replacement buildings, particularly where they are located outside existing settlements.
- In statutorily designated areas they should seek to conserve and enhance the qualities and features that justified the designation.
- Large-scale tourist proposals must be assessed against the whole range of sustainable development objectives. This includes not only their transport implications but also

other sustainability considerations such as how they assist rural regeneration and the well being of communities.

Planning Policy Statement 7 (PPS7) : Sustainable Development in Rural Areas sets out specific national planning policies on tourism and leisure in rural areas.

How to Plan for Tourism

To ensure that their development plans are effective for future development of tourism and thereby provide a framework to make sound planning decisions on tourism proposals, planning authorities should:

- develop and maintain a thorough dialogue with representatives of the tourism industry;
- ensure that this dialogue helps to support a sound data base on the characteristics and needs of tourism in the area; and
- use that data in applying effective techniques designed to ensure that those needs are met as fully as possible.

Involving Stakeholders

It is likely that a large number of groups and individuals will be affected by strategies and proposals for tourism in a particular area. Planners will need to ensure that they have:

- adequately canvassed and considered all of these views;
- in particular, received and understood the views of the community affected and those with a commercial interest in what is proposed; and
- done this at the earliest possible time, in accordance with the principle of 'front-loading' that is an element of the new development plan process.

The Government has issued advice about how the community and other stakeholders should be involved at all stages of the planning process. This is contained in its planning policy statements (PPS) and supporting guidance.

In meeting the requirement to consult business interests, the business interests that they engage are sufficiently wide-ranging and representative of this large and diverse sector. Annex D of PPS identifies potential participants in the RSS revision process. In addition to bodies in that annex that might be consulted to help develop the regional approach to tourism development, specialist tourism organisations

such as the Tourism Alliance, the British Holiday and Homes Parks Association and the group of 'Tourism heads' of the Regional Development Agencies will also be potential consultees.

Key Inputs from the Tourism Industry

Plan-making and review is a continuous process, and this needs to be reflected in the way that stakeholders are consulted and involved. Plan-making bodies should develop constructive dialogues with key players in the tourism sector, and build partnerships with those who have a role in delivery of tourism schemes and programmes.

Above all, there must be constructive and effective engagement with the tourism industry. This will help to ensure that plans are developed with the benefit of a realistic and sustainable commercial perspective, and that those plans relate well to the aspirations of the industry. In particular tourism operators and developers will be able to provide information and views upon:

- tourism markets, levels of demand and planned investment: those making plans for or affecting tourism will need to know what the principal tourism activities in the area are, whether these are growing or declining and if there are any specific types of tourism that the industry is expecting to expand;
- tourism revenues and broader economic impact: plans should be based upon a detailed understanding of the economic value of key tourism sectors and the impacts of these in terms of the number of jobs provided and the services and facilities which are assisted by that tourism activity;
- tourism labour markets: plans for tourism should be based upon information about the number of jobs currently in

tourism, whether these are full-time, levels of skill and of pay. This information will be important to ensure that where plans may change the number or types of tourism jobs, these are realistic in terms of available labour and that they take opportunities to improve the quality and levels of pay for these jobs wherever possible; and

- costs and timings of types of tourism development: where plans propose new tourism development for an area, these should be based upon sound estimates of the cost and timing of this development. This will be necessary in order to ensure that development proposals are realistic and optimal in terms of the expected benefits. Whilst the commercial decision is distinct from the planning process, those responsible for plan-making and implementation are responsible for ensuring that those plans have a good chance of being realised.

Information of this sort will be important in terms of:

- the development of plans at both the regional and local level;
- determining what strategy for tourism is most realistic;
- ascertaining what level of benefits might be expected for local economies and communities; and
- helping support particular proposals, for example to help to demonstrate the benefits of a particular scheme.

Such information will often be complemented, particularly in the urban context, by planning authorities' work on needs assessments for leisure and other town centre uses. Good practice on this process is currently being prepared by Communities and Local Government. It will provide information for forward planning of a wide range of land uses of importance to tourism such as cinemas, restaurants, concert halls, health & fitness clubs, hotels and conference centres.

It is clearly in the interests of the tourism industry to ensure that their aspirations, and particularly their land use requirements, are known and understood by those responsible for drawing up plans. The particular advantages of early and active engagement by the industry and its representatives will be:

- to specify site requirements for inclusion in plans;
- to propose elements of tourism to be included in large scale proposals, such as mixed use and regeneration schemes;
- to comment upon how well the visions and objectives proposed for plans and strategies reflect the aspirations and expectations of the industry; and
- to provide an industry perspective on proposed policies so as to influence their final form.

There are a number of other tourism stakeholders who will similarly need to make an input to emerging plans. Their interests will be broad and include those who control a particular tourism resource (e.g. British Waterways), those seeking to protect the environment (e.g. conservation boards for Areas of Outstanding Natural Beauty) and those supplying a service (e.g. transport operators).

In addition to providing important views, these bodies will often be able to provide information on matters such as:

- the characteristics and attributes of the area which attract tourists, and how these might be protected, developed or enhanced;
- the nature of, and prospects for, transport infrastructure; and
- other existing and emerging plans and investment programmes that are likely to affect the area

Use of Data and Techniques

Data

It is important that strategies and plans for tourism are based upon the best information available. Annex C provides more information about the sources of data and techniques that may assist in planning for tourism. It is for those preparing plans to decide what information they need to gather, and the degree of detail that they will require. To plan effectively for tourism, the following types of information are likely to be required:

- demographic data – drawn from census and other Government sources such as the Labour Force Survey and General Household Survey. This information will be used to establish how many people are employed in different sectors, earnings and qualifications, commuting patterns, skill levels and unemployment levels;
- visitor data – drawn from surveys of tourism behaviour (e.g. Leisure Day Visits Survey, the UK Tourism Survey and the Attractions Survey), statistics from individual tourism attractions, transport operators, area organisations (e.g. National Parks) and hotel occupancy surveys. The information is likely to have already been gathered, but will not always be free to the user. It is useful for establishing seasonal variations and longer term trends in tourism behaviour, which in turn will be important for planning future provision;
- economic studies – these will be used to develop options for particular tourism strategies or to test the business case for a particular tourism development. They may be undertaken by the public or private sector, or a partnership of the two. Such studies are likely to examine how existing patterns of visiting or spending might be influenced by particular initiatives such as the introduction of a new facility, increased bedspaces or new transport links; and
- plans, proposals and programmes – a further reason for consulting a wide range of stakeholders is for the plan-maker to ensure that he has a comprehensive understanding of any relevant programme that may affect tourism in the area and therefore the strategy that he is developing. These initiatives will include the investment plans of tourism operators, statutory undertakers and public bodies, and documents that set out longer term aspirations.

Techniques

Planners will need to consider what methods they need both to access and handle data and in using it to make robust plans and decisions. A clear and methodical approach will be particularly required in respect of:

- community involvement and consultation – including with those who have a commercial interest and those likely to be affected by local changes arising from tourism. This could include:
  * formal written consultation at the outset to establish the nature and extent of local business interests in tourism;
  * focus groups, panels or one-to-one meetings to explore options and support for particular proposals;
  * public meetings and exhibitions to disseminate the plan's vision for tourism and establish the degree of support for those amongst the wider community; and
  * area forums, workshops and 'planning for real' exercises to develop detailed ideas and to promote ownership of the plan's proposals.
- visitor behaviour, including transport choices, use of attractions and accommodation usage. The technique adopted will depend upon why the particular information is being sought. For example, if the development plan is considering whether more overnight accommodation is required in an area, data on use of the current accommodation will be the key requirement. However, patterns of transport use and information about what brings people into the area in the first place will also be important to understand what scope there is for further hotel development and where that could be best located.

When data and techniques are being sought and applied, it is important that those managing and contributing to the process recognise that the same information is likely to be required again at a later date, to assess the plan's progress and effectiveness. So the selection of data and techniques needs to recognise what the ongoing demand upon resources is likely to be. It also means that cooperative working and partnerships need to be nurtured and sustained to enable such monitoring to be readily undertaken.

Key Planning Considerations for Tourism Developments

This section examines some of the key planning issues which may arise in considering proposals for individual tourism developments. The enormous variety of tourism developments mean that the planning considerations will always vary on a case by case basis. However, the following will apply to most developments:

- where the development is located – developments need to be located where they are accessible to visitors (and for many, but not all developments, by means other than just by private car) and where they do not have an adverse impact upon sensitive environments;
- how they are designed – developments should be attractive to users, they need to work well in functional terms and they need to use natural resources in an efficient manner; and
- how they fit into their surroundings – developments need to respect their environs and complement them rather than detract from them. They should be designed to have a positive impact upon landscape, the historical setting and upon ecology.

Choosing the Best Location

In order to be commercially competitive and thus successful, tourism developers will choose sites that are accessible to visitors, and design their developments in such a way that visitors can readily and conveniently enjoy the attraction or facility. The planning authority will share this objective, but in particular will wish to maximise access by sustainable modes of transport, minimise any congestion that the development might give rise to, and ensure that particular sectors of the population are not discouraged from using the attraction when it is completed. Where the attraction or facility is one which lends itself to an urban location, the local planning authority will seek to ensure a town centre location wherever possible.

Planners and developers should work together in order to ensure that new tourism developments are as sustainable as possible in transport terms. At the same time, planners will need to recognise that the wide variety of developments that are inherent in the tourism industry means that there are some developments (e.g. touring sites for caravans) that are car dependent. Wherever possible and feasible for the development concerned, they should look to:

- locate the development close to public transport interchanges and bus routes which will not only help to reduce travel by car but also enable a wider range of people to visit the attraction;
- produce green transport plans – these are often appropriate for larger schemes where there may be scope to reduce private car travel by providing dedicated bus services or greater access by walking or cycling. Park-and-ride provision can be an element of this, as can schemes which provide discounts for those arriving by public transport; and
- establish a visitor management programme– this can be a particularly appropriate solution where an attraction or its surroundings are subject to or the cause of congestion. It may also be advisable where an attraction is fragile or sensitive to use by a large number of people. Visitor management may be achieved by regulating flow (e.g. timed ticket sales) or via development. An example of the latter would be by adding a visitor centre to an historic abbey so that visitors spend less time in the 'fragile', historic part of the site, and more time in the modern, purpose built 'interpretation' building.

There will be some occasions where development for tourism is sought at a location where it will be difficult to meet the objective of access by sustainable modes of transport. The choice of location may have been determined by a functional need, such as in the above example of a visitor centre.

Developers and planners may find that in such cases there will be limited opportunities to make the development accessible by sustainable modes of transport or to reduce the number or proportion of visits made by car.

For small-scale schemes, the traffic generated is likely to be fairly limited and additional traffic movements are therefore unlikely to be a reason for refusal for otherwise suitable tourism developments.

In all cases, planners will need to weigh up the other benefits of a tourism proposal against any disadvantages arising from its location. Some of the key considerations will be the extent to which the proposal:

- helps to protect or improve a specific site or general location. Many new proposals offer the opportunity for landscape enhancement, to re-use an historic building or to improve a derelict and unattractive site;
- contributes to tourism in the locality. New tourism developments will usually be beneficial to the local economy and complement the area's tourism function;
- provides a new facility for the local community as well as visitors;
- assists more generally with diversification of rural economies; and, where appropriate,
- impacts on the vitality and viability of town centres.

Design and Sustainability

Good design is important for tourism because:

- tourism is essentially a commercial activity and its success will depend upon how attractive it is to visitors;
- in areas with many tourist attractions, it is important that each attraction is perceived as contributing to the overall experience; and

- wherever tourist proposals are to be situated, it is important that they complement and improve the wider built and natural environment.

Good design is also a key element in achieving development which is sustainable and will contribute positively towards making places better for people. Developments that are well-designed will be more successful. They will last longer and be more liked. As such they will contribute more to the people who live near or visit them and to the surrounding area as a whole. Further material on design issues can be found in PPS.

Two important aspects of design will be layout and accessibility. Developments that are easy to reach, easy to get around and easy to use are likely to be successful in attracting visitors in the first place and in encouraging them to return. This in turn will assist their commercial success. The details of design are particularly important for tourism because, by definition, visitors are often unfamiliar with the building and its environs. In order to be accessible and used by a wide range of people, tourism developments should be designed to be:

- physically accessible, including to people with impaired mobility and to people with other disabilities such as impaired sight or hearing;
- socially inclusive, facilitating use by all sectors of the community;
- a positive contribution to the host community;
- safe and healthy; and ·attractive.

The careful design of buildings can also make them more sustainable by reducing carbon emissions resulting from their construction and operation. Good energy conservation and using renewable technologies such as wind power and solar gain can reduce the energy needs of buildings and operating costs, whilst improving their sustainability. An important contribution to sustainability can also be made by the selection and use of appropriate materials. Materials from local sources will have less 'embodied energy' (i.e. less fossil fuels will have been taken up transporting and perhaps processing them). Locally-sourced material will also provide local jobs, thus strengthening and diversifying the local economy, and making it more likely that the final development will fit well with the local environment.

The re-use of buildings that have become redundant further improves the overall sustainability of new developments. This also often has the advantage of maintaining important and historic buildings and providing continuity in the landscape and townscape. These sustainable attributes, which may be substantial, may offset certain planning objections to a proposal such as poor location or access.

So, for example, if a hotel was proposed in a redundant building outside of an existing town centre, the decision maker would need to consider and reflect the advantages of the refurbishment proposal against the disadvantage of the less central location.

Contributing to the Environment

Tourism developments may offer considerable opportunities to conserve and enhance the local environment and its inherent qualities. Such advantages will be important considerations in assessing the overall sustainability, and thus acceptability, of a particular proposal. Developers of tourism projects should therefore consider whether new developments can:

- protect and enhance the visual quality of the site and its surroundings, to ensure that the development fits in well with its environs;
- respect the historic interest of the surrounding buildings and areas and ensuring that proposals do not adversely affect the historic environment that people value;
- protect and improve biodiversity. New development should not only protect nature conservation interests (whether it is a statutory requirement or not), but can provide an opportunity to improve biodiversity in an area, for example through the creation of new features of wildlife interest. Such initiatives can complement the wider objectives of tourism developments by increasing the attractiveness of the development to visitors; and

- achieve small-scale improvements to sustainability, for example by recycling waste, using renewable energy and sourcing produce and materials locally.

Determining Tourism Proposals

This section outlines some of the initiatives that developers and planning authorities can take to ensure that proposals for tourism development are processed in an effective and fair manner which will promote optimal outcomes.

Information

Developers can help their proposals to be determined quickly, and achieve a positive outcome, if they provide adequate and appropriate information in support of their applications. For their part local planning authorities need to make clear what information they will be seeking in support of applications for tourism developments. The information required is likely to vary greatly depending on the nature of the proposal, its scale and its location. For larger proposals there may be a wide range of information needed by the planning authority, including:

- the nature of the visits expected to the development, how many they will be, how long and when they will occur;
- what seasonal fluctuation is likely and the extent to which there are expected to be joint trips with other activities in the locality;
- where visits are likely to originate from, and modal split of visitors; and
- the levels of spend and the amount of money expected to be drawn into the local economy.

Developers can help themselves and the local planning authority by seeking discussions with the authority in advance of submitting their planning applications. Such discussions will be an opportunity to identify what information may be required to be submitted in support of the planning application. They will also be helpful in identifying any planning issues and problems and how these might be resolved.

Consultation

Consultation is a statutory requirement and thus an integral part of the planning process. However, there are many potential advantages in going beyond the minimum requirements, particularly through getting the community involved at an early stage in the planning of future developments. Local people are likely to be affected in a number of ways by new tourism proposals. They may be users of a new facility, perhaps even the main users. They may stand to benefit because of jobs or because their businesses may be affected by the presence and operation of the new development.

So there can be distinct advantages in involving local people as their knowledge and opinions will allow adjustments to be made to proposals as they are being developed. This might help in overcoming later objections or help to identify ways of making the proposal more attractive and thus more profitable or successful. The level of consultation with the community should be in proportion to the nature, size and scale of the proposed development.

When undertaking such consultation, it is important that efforts are made to be as inclusive as possible and to understand the needs of groups who might otherwise find it difficult to engage with the planning system. This should include providing the opportunity to put forward ideas and suggestions and to participate in developing proposals and options.

Additional Guidance

One way that local authorities can help developers to draw up schemes that will meet the requirements for new development set out in development plan policies is to provide guidance in advance. This can take a number of forms and will depend upon the characteristics of the area and any particular aims for tourism development that the local plan documents have established.

Where the local planning authority is seeking or expecting considerable tourism development in a number of locations in its area, then it might even be appropriate to draw up a dedicated supplementary planning document on tourism developments to deal with such issues as preferred locations, access, transportation and design.

This document could explain the key objectives for tourism development and seek to ensure that new development supported the overall vision for tourism. Eastbourne has chosen to prepare a supplementary planning document specifically to provide planning advice to developers and others on how the Council will administer its financial viability test for tourist accommodation as set out in the Core Strategy.

Where tourism development is expected just at one or two particular sites within the area, it may be more appropriate to prepare supplementary documents providing design advice to support particular sites allocated in the relevant development plan document. This will help prospective developers to understand the type of development envisaged for the site and how it is expected to integrate physically and functionally with its surroundings.

Another approach might be for the planning authority to provide design guidance for particular types of development, such as for hotels, amusements premises or caravan sites. This will be appropriate where an area has high demand for a particular type of development or when a particular land use is subject to pressures for change or redevelopment.

Compliance with other Statutory Regimes

When planning applications for development are made, the proposals may be subject to other statutory regimes as well. Most planning applications also require approval under building regulations, but there are a range of other statutory requirements that certain developments may need to meet or that developers will need to consider when preparing a planning application for development.

Examples may include the need to obtain listed building or conservation area consent; the need to provide an Environmental Statement to comply with the requirements of the Environmental Impact Assessment (EIA) Regulations; and the need to have regard to the Habitats Regulations, for example in cases where there may be European protected species present on a proposed development site.

Further advice on such matters should be obtained, if necessary, from the local authority before planning applications are submitted.

Using Conditions and Obligations

The granting of planning permission will often be subject to certain conditions being met. These conditions may be used to improve the appearance or functioning of the development or to mitigate against adverse impacts. Conditions must be seen to be fair, reasonable and practicable. For example, typical planning conditions for a tourism or leisure development might:

- regulate the hours during which an attraction could open in order to avoid undue disturbance to people living nearby; or
- require that a caravan site or another type of holiday accommodation be used only for holidays and not as permanent accommodation or as a main residence.

Where it is not possible to include matters in a planning condition, for example where the planning authority wishes to secure on-going management or financial payments, they may seek to negotiate a planning obligation with the developer under section 106 of the Town and Country Planning Act 1990. Obligations must meet certain tests including being directly related to the proposed development and reasonably related in scale and kind to the proposed development.

One example of a tourism-related planning obligation is at the London Wetland Centre where a bus route and terminal have been created and alterations made to cycle lanes. New cycle racks and storage facilities have also been provided, creating a packet of measures that have substantially increased the overall sustainability of this visitor facility.

Tourist Accommodation

1. Tourism accommodation takes many different forms, including hotels, guest houses and bed and breakfast premises, self-catering, touring and static caravans and

camping, and caters for a variety of tastes and budgets. But all are capable of bringing economic benefits to the areas in which they are located. These benefits will need to be assessed alongside other issues such as suitability of the location in terms of its sustainability.

2. The issues that will need to be addressed in considering planning applications for tourist accommodation will vary according to the type, size, and nature of the accommodation being provided. These are considered further below.

Hotel and Serviced Accommodation

General Locational Principles

The process of identifying suitable locations for hotel and serviced accommodation, whatever its nature, should be an integral part of the plan making process. Local planning authorities and the tourist industry should therefore engage constructively to identify suitable locations in plans for hotel accommodation to meet identified current and future needs.

This is particularly important for major hotels – for example those with business, conference and banqueting facilities, or large hotels catering for tourists – where the preference should be to identify town centre sites wherever possible, in line with national policies set out in PPS.

Such sites are the most sustainable in planning terms, since they allow greater access by public transport, contribute to urban vitality and regeneration, and allow visitors to easily access other town centre facilities and attractions. Where proposals for major hotel facilities come forward outside the development plan process, their location should be assessed in line with the policies in PPS and the sequential approach to site selection.

Proposed locations for other types of hotel and serviced accommodation should also be considered through the plan process wherever possible. The emphasis, whatever the type of accommodation, should be on identifying the most sustainable locations, having regard to national planning policies. But in allocating sites in plans, or considering planning applications that come forward outside of the plan process, developers and planning authorities need to recognise that the particular market being met by the accommodation may influence the nature of the location chosen. So, for example, accommodation catering for those seeking to enjoy the natural environment through walking and outdoor recreation may be better located in a rural area, in or at the edge of the centre of a village or small town, rather than in a major town centre some distance away from the attractions it serves.

Whatever the type of hotel or serviced accommodation and whatever its location, it should:

- fit well with its surroundings, having regard to its siting, scale, design, materials and landscaping; and
- be in harmony with the local environment (taking account of, amongst other factors, residential amenity, noise, traffic and parking in the vicinity).

Hotel Accommodation in Rural Areas

National planning policies set out in PPS *Sustainable Development in Rural Areas* makes it clear that the expectation is that most tourism accommodation requiring new buildings should be located in, or adjacent to, existing towns and villages. PPS also recognises that proposals to convert existing rural buildings to provide hotel and other serviced accommodation should be acceptable, subject to any general criteria that may be set in development plans on the re-use of such buildings.

National Parks and Areas of Outstanding Natural Beauty attract visitors who wish to enjoy the special qualities of the landscapes and the countryside of these areas. It is important that sufficient accommodation of a suitable range of types is provided for these visitors.

However, particular care needs to be taken over the number, scale and location of accommodation facilities in these designated areas to ensure that the particular qualities that justified the designation are conserved. These considerations are best addressed through the plan process wherever possible.

Historic Towns and Cities

Historic towns and cities are an attraction to tourists from home and overseas and there is pressure to increase hotel accommodation in them. Great importance is attached to the preservation of buildings of architectural or historic interest both for their intrinsic qualities and for the contribution they make to our towns and villages, and to tourism. It is therefore important that any proposals for new hotel accommodation in such towns and cities are sensitive to their surroundings.

Conversion into hotels is often a realistic proposition for ensuring the retention and maintenance of historic buildings provided it is sensitively handled, does not materially alter the character or historic features of the building, and provided the new use does not generate traffic movements which cannot be accommodated.

Many historic buildings in town and country are already in use as hotels. If carefully designed, additions can be achieved without adversely affecting the historic fabric or character and maintain the historic building in viable use. But large-scale buildings in a small-scale setting, buildings which adversely affect the existing skyline, and those which by their design, materials, illumination or building line are out of sympathy with neighbouring historic buildings will normally be unacceptable.

Modernisation and Extensions

Aside from historic buildings, there are many redundant or semi-obsolete buildings – such as closed mills, distilleries, warehouses, or railway stations – that can lend themselves well to adaptation and modernisation as hotels, other forms of serviced accommodation or restaurants. To convert such buildings to compatible use can bring life back to an otherwise wasted asset– thus conserving a useful and often attractive building, improving a neglected site and helping the local economy.

Similarly, moderate-sized extensions to an existing hotel or public house, including the addition of bedroom accommodation, can help to ensure the future viability of such businesses. This may satisfy a local need as well as a tourism one, by fully utilising the potential of the site but without any disproportionate increase in scale. In all cases, careful consideration should be given to ensure that the size of the extension proposed is not disproportionate for the location concerned.

Budget Hotels, Motels, and Travel Lodges

Where budget hotels are designed to cater for longer stays at a destination (for example, those catering for visitors to historic towns and cities), their location should be considered in light of policies in the development plan and national policies in PPS on town centres. Location of such hotels in town centres maximises the opportunities for visitors to easily access other town centre facilities and attractions.

Other types of budget hotels and similar types of development such as motels and travel lodges cater more for car-born travellers, often for a single overnight stay – e.g. business travellers en-route to a destination. In such cases, the preference of developers will be for sites on major traffic routes outside of the centre of large towns or tourist centres.

However the aim should be to make any development as sustainable as possible, and it will not normally be appropriate for such developments to be located in open countryside away from major settlements. Edge of town centre locations, for example on a ring road or on a major route out of the town centre, will usually be the most appropriate locations if a town centre location is not suitable, available or viable.

For out-of-centre locations, design and layout of the development is likely to be of considerable importance in deciding whether it is acceptable in planning terms. Depending on the setting, an open layout in which careful attention has been paid to achieving a high standard of design and landscaping is likely to be more acceptable than a dense concentration of buildings.

Where a proposal includes other new facilities, such as a petrol station or shop, these will have to be considered on their own merits. If they are objectionable in themselves, the fact that they are combined with a hotel will not remove the objections. Restaurants, fast food outlets, leisure, fitness and other facilities open to the general public as well as residents are also sometimes combined with hotel proposals, in which case the extra traffic they are likely to generate and its effect on the highway must also be taken into account.

Car Parking

Maximum car parking standards for hotel and serviced accommodation may be included in development plans. Where such standards are not included in plans, planning authorities will need to consider what are appropriate levels of parking, based on the market which the hotel serves, its location and availability of public transport facilities.

In addition, for those hotels where a substantial part of the parking needs are attributable to public rooms used mainly for functions which attract non-residents, then the availability of public parking in the vicinity of the hotel will also need to be taken into account.

Planning authorities should also take account of the proposed arrangements for service loading and unloading and setting down space for visitors. Organised tours demand adequate loading and unloading facilities for coaches. Access and waiting areas should be designed with this in mind. Access points should be sited so as to minimise turning movements across traffic and to avoid congestion of the highway caused by vehicles queuing to pick up or drop passengers. Developers should discuss proposed access arrangements with the highway authority at the earliest possible stage.

Holiday, Touring Caravan, and Chalet Parks

In the UK as a whole, the parks industry accounts for tourist spend of some £3.23 billion each year, accommodating some 22% of all holiday bed nights. The industry comprises holiday chalets, caravan holiday homes, pitches for touring caravans, motor-homes and tenting and all types of self-catering accommodation. Holiday parks are the largest provider of rural tourism bed spaces.

PPS. provides advice for planning policies and development proposals for static holiday and touring caravan parks and holiday chalet developments. Planners should carefully weigh the objective of providing adequate facilities and sites with the need to protect landscapes and environmentally sensitive sites.

They should examine the scope for relocating any existing visually or environmentally-intrusive parks away from sensitive areas, or for re-location away from sites prone to flooding or coastal erosion. However, the high land values associated with holiday parks, the cost of infrastructure and possible planning issues relating to a proposed site may make such proposals impractical and unviable.

This advice recognises that planning provides an opportunity to improve the attractiveness of such developments to those who visit them and as features in the landscape.

The *Environmental Code for Holiday parks, Caravan and Camping Sites, and Park Home Estates advises* park owners on fulfilling the industry's commitment to environmental protection. *Holiday Parks: Caring for the Environment – a guide to good practice* (1991), published by the Countryside Commission, remains an important reference document that includes many case studies directing holiday park operators toward best practice. Planners should work with owners and developers of sites to ensure that the most is made of these opportunities. Where there is an identified demand for new or expanded sites, planners should ensure that environmental impacts and impacts on visual amenity are minimised.

New sites that are close to existing settlements and other services will generally be more sustainable as some local services may be accessed by means other than by car. Similarly caravan storage facilities that are close to existing settlements may have less adverse impact and be more sustainable.

However, there may be valid reasons for extending or improving existing holiday parks that are not be located close to existing settlements by virtue of their support for successful local businesses and the provision of employment. Authorities should also consider how the proposal will affect tourism in the area, particularly in terms of its economic and environmental impacts.

Local planning authorities may attach conditions to planning permissions for holiday parks to ensure that they are used for holiday purposes only.

However, with better caravan standards and the trend towards tourism as a year round activity, authorities should give sympathetic consideration to applications to extend the opening period allowed under existing permissions. Annex B covers these matters in more detail.

Staff Accommodation

For many types of holiday parks, a residential managerial presence is often essential, to achieve quality service to the customer, security for the property, and to meet the obligations of health and safety regulations. Accommodation may sometimes also be needed for key members of staff.

As far as possible, suitably located existing dwellings should be used to meet these accommodation needs. But where this is not a feasible option, and particularly in locations where suitable housing is not available, or is unaffordable, it may be necessary to provide new, on-site accommodation for managerial and/or other staff. In such cases the conversion of any suitable available existing buildings should be considered first in preference to the construction of new and potentially intrusive housing development in the countryside.

PPS makes it clear that isolated new houses in the countryside require special justification for planning permission to be granted. PPS further states that one of the few circumstances in which isolated residential development may be justified is when accommodation is required to enable agricultural, forestry and certain other full-time workers to live at, or in the immediate vicinity of their place of work.

There will be some cases where the nature and demands of the work concerned make it essential for one or more people engaged in a tourism enterprise to live at, or very close to, the site of their work. Local planning authorities should give consideration to the essential needs of all businesses located in rural areas, including tourism and should apply the policies set out in PPS–

in particular those in Annex A. Planning conditions can ensure that such accommodation is occupied for this purpose only.

Other Forms of Self-catering Accommodation

PPS advises that local planning authorities should support the provision of other forms of self-catering holiday accommodation in rural areas where this would accord with sustainable development objectives. The re-use and conversion of existing non-residential buildings for this purpose may have added benefits, e.g. as a farm diversification scheme.

Seasonal and Holiday Occupancy Conditions

1. The nature of holidays in this country has become increasingly diverse, in location, in season and in duration. Many people go away several times a year, often for short breaks and not exclusively in the summer months. Much of this demand is for self-catering accommodation – whether in new or converted buildings or in caravan holiday homes. This spread of demand improves the use that is made of this accommodation and so is advantageous to the businesses which provide it and to those host communities which are supported by the spending that it generates. It can help to reduce the disadvantages of seasonal employment, including the difficulties of retaining trained and experienced staff.
2. Whilst extension of the season has these advantages, the demand for this accommodation may occur in areas in which the provision of permanent housing would be contrary to national or local policies which seek to restrict development, for example in order to safeguard the countryside. The planning system can reconcile these two objectives through the use of occupancy conditions designed to ensure that holiday accommodation is used for its intended purpose. Planning authorities commonly impose such conditions when granting permission for self-catering holiday accommodation.
3. One type of condition frequently used for holiday accommodation, particularly in holiday areas, is known

generically as a 'holiday occupancy condition'. The aim of such conditions is generally to ensure that the premises are only used by visitors and do not become part of the local housing stock. There are three principal reasons why a planning authority might seek to do this:

- in order that national or local policies on development of the countryside are not compromised. Often the conversion of redundant rural buildings to holiday accommodation provides a means to retain those buildings without introducing a level of activity that would occur with permanent households;
- to avoid occupation by permanent households which would in turn put pressure upon local services. Permanent households may place demands for local schools and social and health services that would not normally arise from visitors. Moreover, in remote locations the cost of providing these services is greater. It may therefore be reasonable for the planning authority to place an occupancy condition when properties are being built or converted for residential use; and
- to strengthen tourism in a particular area by ensuring that there is a wide range of properties available to encourage visitors to come there on holiday.

Planning authorities will frame these conditions according to local circumstances, and in accordance with general Government advice that conditions should be reasonable and fair. They will also need to frame them so that they can be readily enforced by the authority but in a way that is not unduly intrusive for either owners or occupants.

Another type of condition that may be appropriate for tourist areas is known as a 'seasonal occupancy' condition. This would seek to restrict use of holiday accommodation during particular times of year, perhaps to protect the local environment. This could be used if, for example, use of the premises or the site might affect an important species of bird during its breeding season or when it is winter feeding. Local planning authorities will need to balance the need to impose seasonal occupancy conditions with the wish to avoid exacerbating the seasonal nature of tourism in the locality and its possible adverse effects upon local businesses and jobs.

Data Sources and Techniques

Planners will need to consider relevant quantitative data, including data relating to the economics of tourism development, in both the plan making process and in respect of specific proposals. Development plans (regional spatial strategies and local development frameworks) must be based upon a sound evidence base which has been subject to a rational appraisal. This will need to include an explicit rationale for the vision and strategy for tourism which is being proposed, based in part upon the economic benefits that have been used to justify it.

Local Surveys and Methodologies

Planners may identify a need for local surveys to establish the need for a specific tourist related development. So planners considering hotel accommodation need to have a detailed understanding of the level and demand for accommodation within their area.

Tourism Planning in India

Tourism planning in India started quite late with the first tourism policy being announced by the Government of India in November, 1982 after tourism was recognized as an industry by the Planning Commission of India in June, 1982.

In July, 1986 the Planning Commission of India set up the National Committee on Tourism in order to formulate plans for this sector. The government's initiatives of incorporating a planned tourism sector in India went a long way in boosting Indian tourism.

In May, 1992 the National Action Plan for tourism was announced. The objectives of this landmark plan for tourism planning in India were:

- To improve the economy category domestic tourism
- To develop the tourist areas socially and economically

- To preserve the environment and the national heritage
- To encourage international tourism
- To improve in world tourism India's share
- To increase opportunities for employment in this sector

India tourism planning increased with the seventh five year plan India (1985-1989). The various polices advocated by the seventh plan for tourism planning in India are:

- To promote aggressively domestic tourism
- It laid stress on creating more beach resorts
- To conduct conferences, trekking, conventions, and winter sports so that various options are available to the foreign tourists

These polices of the seventh five year plan gave a boost to the tourism planning India. To further encourage tourism planning in India, the eighth five year plan (1992- 1997) mentioned that the private sector should increase its participation in the sector. The various polices advocated by the eighth plan for tourism planning in India are:

- To develop the tourists places
- To develop winter sports, beach resort, and wildlife tourism
- To restore the projects of national heritage
- To provide in tourists centres economy class accommodation

Tourism planning in India has increased by leaps and bounds in the last few years and the government and Department of Tourism needs to make continuous efforts to ensure that tourism planning in India takes the tourism sector of the country to greater heights on a sustainable basis.

Ecotourism and the Tourism Industry

Ecotourism

'Ecotourism' (also known as ecological tourism) is responsible travel to fragile, pristine, and usually protected areas that strives

to be low impact and (often) small scale. It purports to educate the traveller; provide funds for conservation; directly benefit the economic development and political empowerment of local communities; and foster respect for different cultures and for human rights.

Eco tourism is held as important by those who participate in it so that future generations may experience aspects of the environment relatively untouched by human intervention. Most serious studies of ecotourism including several university programs now use this as the working definition.

Ecotourism appeals to ecologically and socially conscious individuals. Generally speaking, it focuses on volunteering, personal growth and environmental responsibility. It typically involves travel to destinations where flora, fauna, and cultural heritage are the primary attractions. One of the goals of ecotourism is to offer tourists insight into the impact of human beings on the environment, and to foster a greater appreciation of our natural habitats.

Responsible ecotourism includes programs that minimize the negative aspects of conventional tourism on the environment and enhance the cultural integrity of local people. Therefore, in addition to evaluating environmental and cultural factors, an integral part of ecotourism is the promotion of recycling, energy efficiency, water conservation, and creation of economic opportunities for local communities.

Criteria

Ecotourism is a form of tourism that involves travelling to tranquil and unpolluted natural areas. According to the definition and principles of ecotourism established by The International Ecotourism Society (TIES) in 1990, ecotourism is "Responsible travel to natural areas that conserves the environment and improves the well-being of local people." (TIES, 1990). Martha Honey, expands on the TIES definition by describing the seven characteristics of ecotourism, which are:

- Involves travel to natural destinations.
- Minimizes impact.

- Builds environmental awareness.
- Provides direct financial benefits for conservation.
- Provides financial benefits and empowerment for local people.
- Respects local culture.
- Supports human rights and democratic movements.

Ideally, ecotourism should satisfy several criteria, such as:

- conservation of biological diversity and cultural diversity through ecosystem protection
- promotion of sustainable use of biodiversity, by providing jobs to local populations
- sharing of socioeconomic benefits with local communities and indigenous peoples by having their informed consent and participation in the management of ecotourism enterprises
- tourism to unspoiled natural resources, with minimal impact on the environment being a primary concern.
- minimization of tourism's own environmental impact
- affordability and lack of waste in the form of luxury
- local culture, flora and fauna being the main attractions.

For many countries, ecotourism is not simply a marginal activity to finance protection of the environment, but is a major industry of the national economy. For example, in Costa Rica, Ecuador, Nepal, Kenya, Madagascar and Antarctica, ecotourism represents a significant portion of the gross domestic product and economic activity.

The concept of ecotourism is widely misunderstood and in practice is often used as a marketing tool to promote tourism that is related to nature. This is an especially frequent malpractice in the realm of Jungle tourism. Critics claim that these greenwashing practices, carried out in the name of ecotourism, often consist of placing a hotel in a splendid landscape, to the detriment of the ecosystem. According to them, ecotourism must above all sensitize people to the beauty and the fragility of nature. They condemn some operators as greenwashing their operations: using the labels of "green" and "eco-friendly", while behaving in environmentally irresponsible ways. Although academics disagree about who can be classified as an ecotourist and there is little statistical data, some estimate that more than five million ecotourists - the majority of the ecotourist population - come from the United States, with many others from Western Europe, Canada and Australia.

Currently, there are various moves to create national and international ecotourism accreditation programs, although the process is also controversial. National ecotourism certification programs have been put in place in countries such as Costa Rica, Australia, Kenya and Sweden.

History

Ecotourism, responsible tourism, jungle tourism, and sustainable development have become prevalent concepts since the late 1980s, and ecotourism has experienced arguably the fastest growth of all sub-sectors in the tourism industry.

The popularity represents a change in tourist perceptions, increased environmental awareness, and a desire to explore natural environments. At times, such changes become as much a statement affirming one's social identity, educational sophistication, and disposable income as it has about preserving the Amazon rainforest or the Caribbean reef for posterity.

Criticisms

Definitional Problems and Greenwashing

To approach an understanding of the problem, a clear definition must delineate what is, and is not, ecotourism. Ideally, ecotourism satisfies several general criteria, including the conservation of biological diversity and cultural diversity through ecosystem protection, promotion of sustainable use of biodiversity, share of social-economic benefits with local communities through informed consent and participation, increase in environmental and cultural knowledge, affordability and reduced waste, and minimization of its own environmental impact. In such ways, it contributes to the long term benefits to both the environment and local communities.

However, in the continuum of tourism activities that stretch from conventional tourism to ecotourism proper, there has been a lot of contention to the limit at which biodiversity preservation, local social-economic benefits, and environmental impact can be considered "ecotourism".

For this reason, environmentalists, special interest groups, and governments define ecotourism differently. Environmental organizations have generally insisted that ecotourism is nature-based, sustainably managed, conservation supporting, and environmentally educated.

The tourist industry and governments, however, focus more on the product aspect, treating ecotourism as equivalent to any sort of tourism based in nature. As a further complication, many terms are used under the rubric of ecotourism. Nature tourism, low impact tourism, green tourism, bio-tourism, ecologically responsible tourism, and others have been used in literature and marketing, although they are not necessary synonymous with ecotourism.

The problems associated with defining ecotourism have led to confusion among tourists and academics alike. Definitional problems are also subject of considerable public controversy and concern because of green washing, a trend towards the commercialization of tourism schemes disguised as sustainable, nature based, and environmentally friendly ecotourism.

According to McLaren, these schemes are environmentally destructive, economically exploitative, and culturally insensitive at its worst. They are also morally disconcerting because they mislead tourists and manipulate their concerns for the environment. Despite objections, green washing continues to grow unabated.

The Nature's Sacred Paradise, a theme park in Quintana Roo, Mexico, is responsible for displacing local Mayan communities and illegally keeping endangered species in captivity to attract visitors. The development and success of such large scale, energy intensive, and ecologically unsustainable schemes are a testament to the tremendous profits associated with being labeled as ecotourism.

Negative Impact of Tourism

Ecotourism has become one of the fastest-growing sectors of the tourism industry, growing annually by 10-15% worldwide (Miller, 2007). One definition of ecotourism is "the practice of low-impact, educational, ecologically and culturally sensitive travel that benefits local communities and host countries" (Honey, 1999). Many of the ecotourism projects are not meeting these standards.

Even if some of the guidelines are being executed, the local communities are still facing other negative impacts. South Africa is one of the countries that are reaping significant economic benefits from ecotourism, but negative effects - including forcing people to leave their homes, gross violations of fundamental rights, and environmental hazards - far outweigh the medium-term economic benefits (Miller, 2007).

A tremendous amount of money is being spent and human resources continue to be used for ecotourism despite unsuccessful outcomes, and even more money is put into public relation campaigns to dilute the effects of criticism. Ecotourism channels resources away from other projects that could contribute more sustainable and realistic solutions to pressing social and environmental problems. "The money tourism can generate often ties parks and managements to ecotourism" (Walpole et al. 2001). But there is a tension in this relationship because ecotourism often causes conflict and changes in land-use rights, fails to deliver promises of community-level benefits, damages environments, and has plenty of other social impacts.

Indeed many argue repeatedly that ecotourism is neither ecologically nor socially beneficial, yet it persists as a strategy for conservation and development (West, 2006). While several studies are being done on ways to improve the ecotourism structure, some argue that these examples provide rationale for stopping it altogether.

The ecotourism system exercises tremendous financial and political influence. The evidence above shows that a strong case exists for restraining such activities in certain locations. Funding could be used for field studies aimed at finding alternative solutions to tourism and the diverse problems Africa faces in result of urbanization, industrialization, and the over exploitation of agriculture (Kamuaro, 2007). At the local level, ecotourism has become a source of conflict over control of land, resources, and tourism profits. In this case, ecotourism has harmed the environment and local people, and has led to conflicts over profit distribution.

In a perfect world more efforts would be made towards educating tourists of the environmental and social effects of their travels. Very few regulations or laws stand in place as boundaries for the investors in ecotourism. These should be implemented to prohibit the promotion of unsustainable ecotourism projects and materials which project false images of destinations, demeaning local and indigenous cultures.

Direct Environmental Impacts

Ecotourism operations occasionally fail to live up to conservation ideals. It is sometimes overlooked that ecotourism is a highly consumer-centred activity, and that environmental conservation is a means to further economic growth.

Although ecotourism is intended for small groups, even a modest increase in population, however temporary, puts extra pressure on the local environment and necessitates the development of additional infrastructure and amenities.

The construction of water treatment plants, sanitation facilities, and lodges come with the exploitation of non-renewable energy sources and the utilization of already limited local resources. The conversion of natural land to such tourist infrastructure is implicated in deforestation and habitat deterioration of butterflies in Mexico and squirrel monkeys in Costa Rica. In other cases, the environment suffers because local communities are unable to meet the infrastructure demands of ecotourism. The lack of adequate sanitation facilities in many East African parks results in the disposal of campsite sewage in rivers, contaminating the wildlife, livestock, and people who draw drinking water from it.

Aside from environmental degradation with tourist infrastructure, population pressures from ecotourism also leaves behind garbage and pollution associated with the Western lifestyle.

Although ecotourists claim to be educationally sophisticated and environmentally concerned, they rarely understand the ecological consequences of their visits and how their day-to-day activities append physical impacts on the environment.

As one scientist observes, they "rarely acknowledge how the meals they eat, the toilets they flush, the water they drink, and so on, are all part of broader regional economic and ecological systems they are helping to reconfigure with their very activities." Nor do ecotourists recognize the great consumption of non-renewable energy required to arrive at their destination, which is typically more remote than conventional tourism destinations. For instance, an exotic journey to a place 10,000 kilometres away consumes about 700 litres of fuel per person.

Ecotourism activities are, in of itself, issues in environmental impact because they disturb fauna and flora. Ecotourists believe that because they are only taking pictures and leaving footprints, they keep ecotourism sites pristine, but even harmless sounding activities such as a nature hike can be ecologically destructive.

In the Annapurna Circuit in Nepal, ecotourists have worn down the marked trails and created alternate routes, contributing to soil impaction, erosion, and plant damage. Where the ecotourism activity involves wildlife viewing, it can scare away animals, disrupt their feeding and nesting sites, or acclimate them to the presence of people. In Kenya, wildlife-observer disruption drives cheetahs off their reserves, increasing the risk of inbreeding and further endangering the species.

Environmental Hazards

Unfortunately, industrialization, urbanization, and unsustainable agriculture practices have all had serious effects on the environment. Ecotourism is now also playing a role in this depletion. While the term ecotourism may sound relatively benign, one of its most serious impacts is its consumption of virgin territories (Kamuaro, 2007).

These invasions often include deforestation, disruption of ecological life systems and various forms of pollution, all of which contribute to environmental degradation. The number of motor vehicles crossing the park increases as tour drivers search for rare species. The number of roads has disrupted the grass cover which has serious effects on plant and animal species. These areas also have a higher rate of disturbances and invasive species because of all the traffic moving off the beaten path into new undiscovered areas (Kamuaro, 2007). Ecotourism also has an effect on species through the value placed on them. "Certain species have gone from being little known or valued by local people to being highly valued commodities. The commodification of plants may erase their social value and lead to overproduction within protected areas. Local people and their images can also be turned into commodities" (West, 2006). Kamuaro brings up a relatively obvious contradiction, any commercial venture into unspoiled, pristine land with or without the "eco" prefix as a contradiction in terms. To generate revenue you have to have a high number of traffic, tourists, which inevitably means a higher pressure on the environment.

Local People

Most forms of ecotourism are owned by foreign investors and corporations that provide few benefits to local communities. An overwhelming majority of profits are put into the pockets of investors instead of reinvestment into the local economy or environmental protection. The limited numbers of local people who are employed in the economy enter at its lowest level, and are unable to live in tourist areas because of meager wages and a two market system.

In some cases, the resentment by local people results in environmental degradation. As a highly publicized case, the Masai nomads in Kenya killed wildlife in national parks to show aversion to unfair compensation terms and displacement from traditional lands. The lack of economic opportunities for local people also constrains them to degrade the environment as a means of sustenance. The presence of affluent ecotourists encourage the development of destructive markets in wildlife souvenirs, such as the sale of coral trinkets on tropical islands and animal products in Asia, contributing to illegal harvesting and poaching from the environment. In Suriname, sea turtle reserves use a large portion of their budget to guard against these destructive activities.

Displacement of People

One of the most powerful examples of communities being moved in order to create a park is the story of the Masai. About 70% of national parks and game reserves in East Africa are on Masai land (Kamuaro, 2007). The first undesirable impact of tourism was that of the extent of land lost from the Masai culture. Local and national governments took advantage of the Masai's ignorance on the situation and robbed them of huge chunks of grazing land, putting to risk their only socioeconomic livelihood. In Kenya the Masai also have not gained any economic benefits. Despite the loss of their land, employment favours better educated workers. Furthermore the investors in this area are not local and have not put profits back into local economy. In some cases game reserves can be created without informing or consulting local people, who come to find out about the situation when an eviction notice is delivered (Kamuaro, 2007). Another source of resentment is the manipulation of the local people by their government. "Ecotourism works to create simplistic images of local people and their uses and understandings of their surroundings. Through the lens of these simplified images, officials direct policies and projects towards the local people and the local people are blamed if the projects fail" (West, 2006). Clearly tourism as a trade is not empowering the local people who make it rich and satisfying. Instead ecotourism exploits and depletes, particularly in African Masai tribes. It has to be reoriented if it is to be useful to local communities and to become sustainable (Kamuaro, 2007).

Threats to Indigenous Cultures

Ecotourism often claims that it preserves and "enhances" local cultures. However, evidence shows that with the establishment of protected areas local people have illegally lost their homes, and most often with no compensation (Kamuaro, 2007). Pushing people onto marginal lands with harsh climates, poor soils, lack of water, and infested with livestock and disease does little to enhance livelihoods even when a proportion of ecotourism profits are directed back into the community.

The establishment of parks can create harsh survival realities and deprive the people of their traditional use of land and natural resources. Ethnic groups are increasingly being seen as a "backdrop" to the scenery and wildlife.

The local people struggle for cultural survival and freedom of cultural expression while being "observed" by tourists. Local indigenous people also have strong resentment towards the change, "Tourism has been allowed to develop with virtually no controls. Too many lodges have been built, too much firewood is being used and no limits are being placed on tourism vehicles. They regularly drive off-track and harass the wildlife. Their vehicle tracks criss-cross the entire Masai Mara. Inevitably the bush is becoming eroded and degraded" (Kamuaro, 2007).

Mismanagement

While governments are typically entrusted with the administration and enforcement of environmental protection, they often lack the commitment or capability to manage ecotourism sites effectively. The regulations for environmental protection may be vaguely defined, costly to implement, hard to enforce, and uncertain in effectiveness.

Government regulatory agencies, as political bodies, are susceptible to making decisions that spend budget on politically beneficial but environmentally unproductive projects. Because of prestige and conspicuousness, the construction of an attractive visitor's center at an ecotourism site may take precedence over more pressing environmental concerns like acquiring habitat, protecting endemic species, and removing invasive ones. Finally, influential groups can pressure and sway the interests of the government to their favour. The government and its regulators can become vested in the benefits of the ecotourism industry which they are supposed to regulate, causing restrictive environmental regulations and enforcement to become more lenient.

Management of ecotourism sites by private ecotourism companies offers an alternative to the cost of regulation and deficiency of government agencies. It is believed that these companies have a self interest in limited environmental degradation, because tourists will pay more for pristine environments, which translates to higher profit. However, theory indicates that this practice is not economically feasible and will fail to manage the environment. The model of monopolistic competition states that distinctiveness will entail profits, but profits will promote imitation. A company that protects its ecotourism sites is able to charge a premium for the novel experience and pristine environment. But when other companies view the success of this approach, they also enter the market with similar practices, increasing competition and reducing demand. Eventually, the demand will be reduced until the economic profit is zero. A cost-benefit analysis shows that the company bears the cost of environmental protection without receiving the gains. Without economic incentive, the whole premise of self interest through environmental protection is quashed; instead, ecotourism companies will minimize environment related expenses and maximize tourism demand.

The tragedy of the commons offers another model for economic unsustainability from environmental protection, in ecotourism sites utilized by many companies. Although there is a communal incentive to protect the environment, maximizing the benefits in the long run, a company will conclude that it is in their best interest to utilize the ecotourism site beyond its sustainable level. By increasing the number of ecotourists, for instance, a company gains all the economic benefit while paying only a part of the environmental cost. In the same way, a company recognizes that there is no incentive to actively protect the environment; they bear all the costs, while the benefits are shared by all other companies. The result, again, is mismanagement.

Taken together, the mobility of foreign investment and lack of economic incentive for environmental protection means that ecotourism companies are disposed to establishing themselves in new sites once their existing one is sufficiently degraded.

World Tourism Statistics and Rankings

Most Visited Countries by International Tourist Arrivals

The World Tourism Organization reports the following ten countries as the most visited in between 2006 and 2008 by number of international travellers. When compared to 2006, Ukraine entered the top ten list, surpassing Russia, Austria and Mexico, and in 2008 surpassed Germany. In 2008 the U.S. displaced Spain from the second place. Most of the top visited countries continue to be on the European continent.

International Tourism Receipts

In 2008, there were over 922 million international tourist arrivals, with a growth of 1.9% as compared to 2007. International tourism receipts grew to US$944 billion (euro 642 billion) in 2008, corresponding to an increase in real terms of 1.8% on 2007. When the export value of international passenger transport receipts is accounted for, total receipts in 2008 reached a record of US$1.1 trillion, or over US$3 billion a day.

International Tourism Expenditures

The World Tourism Organization reports the following countries as the top ten biggest spenders on international tourism for the year 2008. For the fifth year in a row, German tourists continue as the top spenders.

History

Wealthy people have always travelled to distant parts of the world, to see great buildings, works of art, learn new languages, experience new cultures and to taste different cuisines. Long ago, at the time of the Roman Republic, places such as Baiae were popular coastal resorts for the rich. The word *tourism* was used by 1811 and *tourist* by 1840. In 1936, the League of Nations defined *foreign tourist* as "someone travelling abroad for at least twenty-four hours". Its successor, the United Nations, amended this definition in 1945, by including a maximum stay of six months.

Leisure Travel

Leisure travel was associated with the Industrial Revolution in the United Kingdom – the first European country to promote leisure time to the increasing industrial population. Initially, this applied to the owners of the machinery of production, the economic oligarchy, the factory owners and the traders. These comprised the new middle class. Cox & Kings was the first official travel company to be formed in 1758. The British origin of this new industry is reflected in many place names. In Nice, France, one of the first and best-established holiday resorts on the French Riviera, the long esplanade along the seafront is known to this day as the *Promenade des Anglais*; in many other historic resorts in continental Europe, old, well-established palace hotels have names like the *Hotel Bristol*, the *Hotel Carlton* or the *Hotel Majestic* – reflecting the dominance of English customers.

Many leisure-oriented tourists travel to the tropics, both in the summer and winter. Places often visited are: Cuba, the Dominican Republic, Thailand, North Queensland in Australia and Florida in the United States.

Winter Tourism

Major ski resorts are located in the various European countries (e.g. Austria, Bulgaria, Czech Republic, France, Germany, Iceland, Italy, Norway, Poland, Sweden, Slovakia, Spain, Switzerland), Canada, the United States, Australia, New Zealand, Japan, South Korea, Chile and Argentina.

Mass Tourism

Mass tourism could only have developed with the improvements in technology, allowing the transport of large numbers of people in a short space of time to places of leisure interest, so that greater numbers of people could begin to enjoy the benefits of leisure time. In the United States, the first seaside resorts in the European style were at Atlantic City, New Jersey and Long Island, New York.

In Continental Europe, early resorts included: Ostend, popularized by the people of Brussels; Boulogne-sur-Mer (Pas-de-Calais) and Deauville (Calvados) for the Parisians; and Heiligendamm, founded in 1797, as the first seaside resort on the Baltic Sea.

Mountainous Regions of Central Asia and in the Himalayas

Tourism is coming to the previously isolated but spectacular mountainous regions of Central Asia, the Hindu Kush and the Himalayas. Closed for so many years to visitors from abroad, it now attracts a growing number of foreign tourists by its unique culture and splendid natural beauty. However, while this influx of tourists is bringing economic opportunities and employment to local populations, helping to promote these little-known regions of the world, it has also brought challenges along with it: to ensure that it is well-managed and that its benefits are shared by all.

As a response to this concern, the Norwegian Government, as well as the UNESCO, organized an interdisciplinary project called the Development of Cultural and Ecotourism in the Mountainous Regions of Central Asia and the Himalayas project. It aims to establish links and promote cooperation between local communities, national and international NGOs, and tour agencies in order to heighten the role of the local community and involve them fully in the employment opportunities and income-generating activities that tourism can bring. Project activities include training local tour guides, producing high-quality craft items and promoting home-stays and bed-and-breakfast type accommodation.

As of now, the project is drawing on the expertise of international NGOs and tourism professionals in the seven participating countries, making a practical and positive contribution to alleviating poverty by helping local communities to draw the maximum benefit from their region's tourism potential, while protecting the environmental and cultural heritage of the region concerned.

The University of TRAVELHOST, Dallas, Texas has an extensive travel library continually gathering travel related research and tourism economic impact studies nationwide.

Space Tourism

Space tourism is the phenomenon of tourists paying for flights into space. As of 2009, orbital space tourism opportunities are limited and expensive, with only the Russian Space Agency providing transport. The price for a flight brokered by Space Adventures to the International Space Station aboard a Soyuz spacecraft is US$20–35 million. The space tourists usually sign contracts with third parties to conduct certain research while in orbit. This helps to minimize their own expenses.

Infrastructure for a suborbital space tourism industry is being developed through the construction of spaceports in numerous locations, including California, Oklahoma, New Mexico, Florida, Virginia, Alaska, Wisconsin, Esrange in Sweden as well as the

United Arab Emirates. Some use the term "personal spaceflight" as in the case of the Personal Spaceflight Federation.

A number of startup companies have sprung up in recent years, hoping to create a space tourism industry. For a list of such companies, and the spacecraft they are currently building, see list of space tourism companies.

Russia announced on 3 March 2010 that they would be ending their space tourism program, at least for the next several years.

Dark Tourism

Dark tourism (also black tourism or grief tourism) is tourism involving travel to sites associated with death and suffering. Thanatourism, derived from the Ancient Greek word *thanatos* for the personification of death, is associated with dark tourism but refers more specifically to violent death; it is used in fewer contexts than the terms dark tourism, grief tourism, and quite tourism.

This includes castles and battlefields such as Culloden near Inverness, Scotland, Chernobyl in ex USSR, or Bran Castle, Poienari Castle in Romania; sites of disaster, either natural or man made such as Ground Zero in New York; prisons now open to the public such as Beaumaris Prison in Anglesey, Wales; and purpose built centers such as the London Dungeon. A notable example is how tourism to Detroit is sometimes geared towards looking at the fall of the former glamor instead of what it has managed to retain.

The best-known destination for dark tourism is the German extermination camp at Auschwitz in Poland.

Index

K

L

M

N

O

P

Q

R

□□□